21 terrific patchwork bags

Susan Briscoe

David & Charles

Susan Briscoe studied Visual Art and Drama at the University College of Wales before moving to Japan to teach English. With an interest in costume and textiles, Susan studied kimono making but became hooked on Japanese fabrics allied with their patchwork and quilting techniques. On her return to Wales she succeeded in combining her design and needlework skills with a need for practical accessories in her job as a footpath officer.

Susan now writes and designs for patchwork and needlecraft magazines and teaches bag making and sashiko quilting. She has exhibited at UK national quilting shows as well as in Japan.

For my mum, who started me sewing.

Photograph on page 1
A wonderful set of workbags, specially designed with quilters in mind: a long workbag (front), a quilter's briefcase (centre), a small workbag (centre in pocket) and a quilter's travel bag (back).

A DAVID & CHARLES BOOK
Copyright © David & Charles Limited 2003, 2005

David & Charles is an F+W Publications Inc. company
4700 East Galbraith Road
Cincinnati, OH 45236

First published in the UK in 2003
Reprinted 2004
First US paperback edition 2003
Reprinted 2003, 2004 (twice)
First UK paperback edition 2005
Reprinted 2006

Text Copyright © Susan Briscoe 2003, 2005
Photography and layout Copyright © David & Charles 2003, 2005

A catalogue record for this book is available from the British Library.

ISBN-13: 978-0-7153-1440-1 hardback
ISBN-10: 0-7153-1440-8 hardback

ISBN-13: 978-0-7153-1443-2 paperback
ISBN-10: 0-7153-1443-2 paperback

Printed in Singapore by KHL Printing Co Pte Ltd
for David & Charles
Brunel House   Newton Abbot   Devon

Visit our website at www.davidandcharles.co.uk

David & Charles books are available from all good bookshops; alternatively you can contact our Orderline on 0870 9908222 or write to us at FREEPOST EX2 110, D&C Direct, Newton Abbot, TQ12 4ZZ (no stamp required UK only); US customers call 800-289-0963 and Canadian customers call 800-840-5220.

Contents

Introduction	4
Using this book	5
Envelope Bag	6
Tough Tote	12
Double Bottle Bag	18
Quilter's Travel Bag	24
Victorian Circle Bag	30
Long Workbag	36
Quilter's Briefcase	42
Small Workbag	50
Fan Purse	56
Rice Sack Bag	62
Inside Outside Bag	70
Batik Satchel	76
Zipover Rucksack	82
Equipment and Materials	88
Patchwork Techniques	95
Quilting Techniques	103
Bag Making Techniques	106
Stitch Library	112
Fabric Themes	114
Block Library	116
Suppliers	120
Acknowledgments	120
Index	121

Introduction

Bags are a great way to show off your patchwork and quilting skills, whether you are a beginner or an experienced quilter. You can travel with a co-ordinated set of quilter's work bags, accessorize your evening outfit with a beautiful purse, go shopping, walking or whatever you like. They also make great gifts – if you can bear to give them away!

Whatever your level of ability, you can use this book to make a variety of practical and pretty bags. There are step-by-step instructions for each bag and a section covering all the basics of patchwork and quilting you need for the projects. The bags were chosen for versatility. They are ideal for trying out new techniques and patchwork blocks, revisiting old favourites in new fabrics or using up blocks left over from larger quilts. As small projects they use small amounts of fabric and wadding (batting), so you can use scraps too. Even some fabrics unsuitable for patchwork can be used for the plain sections of the bags. They are quick and satisfying to make – and fun to use!

Practicality and durability are as important as good looks. I wanted to make bags that could be used every day, as well as for special occasions. So the parts that need to be tough are tough, such as straps and bases, and the fancy bits can be as fancy as you like – why not express your individuality and embellish your quilting with embroidery, beads and buttons as the mood takes you?

When I designed the bags, I considered the best features of my favourite bags and useful additions. The patterns can be adapted to suit your personal needs and preferences and there is also a library of patchwork blocks to choose from, offering you further inspiration. The detailed instructions show you how to make the bags as I did or you can pick and mix, changing the designs as you like. Various methods for making pockets, straps and fastenings are described throughout the projects so every bag you make can be unique.

Enjoy stitching!

Using this Book

The following are useful points about using this book, even for experienced quilters – please read before making any project. Those who need further information on equipment, materials and techniques will find all they need to know in the resource section beginning on page 88.

▶ Fabric pieces and patchwork blocks are given *without* seam allowances, unless stated otherwise, so add a ¼in seam allowance all round. Add ½in seam allowance to edges of openings where zips will be inserted.

▶ Wadding (batting) and backing fabric sizes are also given without seam allowances, so add seam allowances as above for the minimum size. It is usually easier to cut wadding and backing larger than required and trim to size after quilting.

▶ Actual sizes are given for cord, braid, zips and so on. There is no need to add on any extra allowance.

▶ 'Machine sew' means with straight stitch, unless otherwise stated. Start and finish all bag construction seams by reverse stitching for ½in.

▶ Where possible patchwork blocks in the projects are actual size but check individual diagrams for the size required.

▶ Press seams after sewing each stage of patchwork and bag assembly. Where patchwork is sewn to a plain panel, press seams away from the patchwork.

▶ Illustrations of stitches used are to be found in the Stitch Library on page 112.

▶ Alternate patchwork blocks are supplied in the Block Library on page 116.

Envelope Bag

What could be simpler than this charming little bag? It would make a perfect bridesmaid's accessory or a delightful evening bag for a special occasion. I combined scraps of silk bridal fabrics with gold prints and embellished it with machine embroidery, although hand embroidery would produce an equally gorgeous effect. The usual Log Cabin dark/light effect was replaced with a subtle silk/print contrast. Folded from one piece of lined patchwork and oversewn by hand, it's so easy to make and looks so pretty, you could make it from any square of patchwork. The cord strap and button loop are sewn in with the lining. I used a heart-shaped, mother-of-pearl button to complete the romantic theme.

You Will Need

Add seam allowances to all fabric and wadding sizes – see page 5

- Four 5in square Log Cabin patchwork blocks in scraps of printed cottons and silk
- Backing fabric 10in square
- 2oz cotton wadding (batting) 10in square
- Lining fabric 10in square
- One 2in square to match lining, cut on bias
- Medium cord 55in long for strap

- Decorative button (with shank)
- Fine cord or narrow ribbon for button loop
- Sewing thread to tone with patchwork fabrics
- Shaded machine embroidery thread for quilting
- Metallic machine needle and embroidery machine needle

Making the Patchwork

1 Begin by making the four 5in Log Cabin blocks, using the pattern given in **Fig 1** and following the instructions on page 100. The block centres are cream/white silk. Use pastel silk fabrics for dark shades and gold prints for the light tints.

2 Make the bag panel by grouping the four Log Cabin blocks together using **Fig 2** as a guide (note the layout of the light and dark areas in the blocks). Using the wadding (batting) and backing fabric, sandwich, and quilt (see making a quilt sandwich, page 103). Quilt along the centre of the strips, using machine or hand embroidery stitches (see machine quilting page 103 and the Stitch Library page 112).

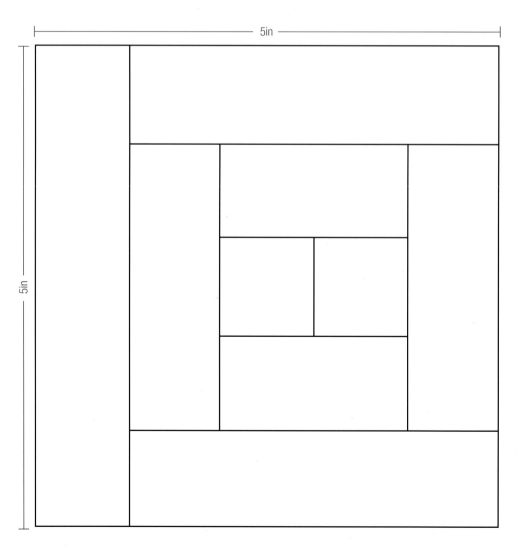

Fig 1 Log Cabin block (actual size) – make 4 the same

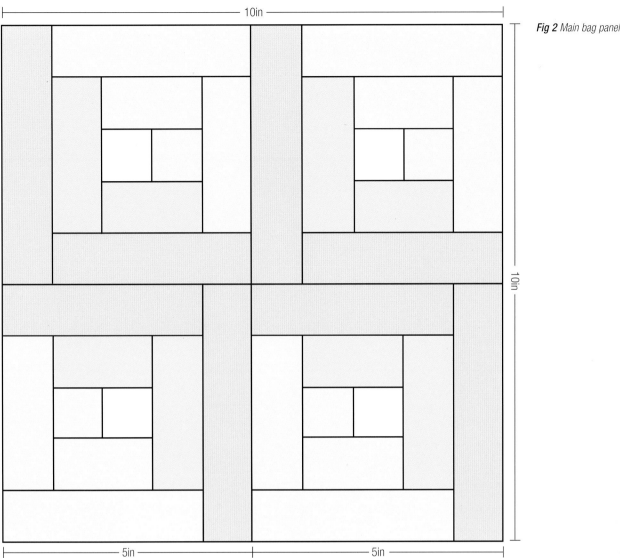

10in

10in

5in 5in

Fig 2 Main bag panel – make 1

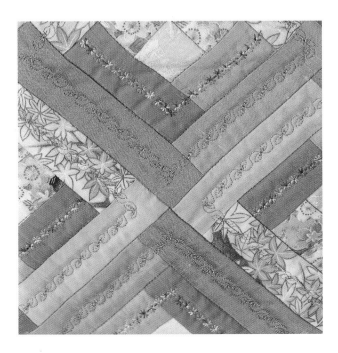

tip

Unlike patchwork cottons, most silks should not be washed, as it may dull their finish or shrink them. If you want to be able to wash your bag, replace the silks with satin ribbons.

Constructing the Bag

3 Tack (baste) the cord strap and button loop in place on the bag panel, angling them as shown in the photograph.

4 With right sides together, machine sew the lining to the bag panel, leaving a gap approximately 3in unsewn for turning.

5 Clip the corners off the bag panel, approximately ⅛in, being careful not to cut too close to the corner stitching. Turn the bag panel right side out through the gap left in the stitching, making sure that the panel corners are well turned out. Slipstitch the gap closed.

6 With the bag panel patchwork side up, fold up the bottom corner point and one side corner point to meet. Starting where the two corner points meet, oversew (whipstitch) together, stitching through the lining fabric only. This produces an attractive effect – a narrow strip of lining fabric visible on the front of the bag. Start and finish by oversewing in the opposite direction for about ½in. Repeat for the other side of bag.

tip ▶▶▶ *Remember the straight grain runs parallel to the fabric selvage and, unlike the crosswise grain, does not tend to stretch. If your triangle stretches along the top fold, unpick it, fold on the opposite diagonal and re-sew.*

7 Fold the 2in bias-cut fabric square right sides together to make a triangle, so the straight grain of the fabric is running along the longest side of the triangle. Machine sew along the edges of triangle, leaving a gap approximately 1in unsewn. Clip the corners and turn right side out. Slipstitch the gap closed. Oversew the triangle panel to the V-shaped space in front of the bag. To finish, sew on the button.

idea *This is the ideal opportunity to use a single precious or antique button. If your button is crystal or glass, why not enhance your bag with a scattering of embroidery beads for extra sparkle?*

Variation

This fun rainbow bag was made with 7in Log Cabin blocks, hand quilted along each strip with rainbow-shaded perlé thread. Deep purple textured prints set off the bright colours well with a strong dark/bright contrast. For a casual effect, I used a popper fastener. The rainbow cord strap is threaded through eyelets and the centre join is hidden and strengthened by a strip of wadding (batting) and fabric wrapped around the cord. This shoulder padding makes the bag more comfortable to carry than cord alone.

Tough Tote

A strong everyday tote bag is just what's needed to shop in style, even if I'm only going to the supermarket for bread! The bottom of the bag is cut from one piece of strong denim sewn into a box shape. Contrasting piping protects the corners and the strong webbing strap forms a continuous loop to help carry heavier groceries. The centres of the Canadian Gardens variation blocks are miniature scenes from a toile de Jouy print. Fair and Square, another traditional block, complements the design and machine quilting sharpens up the geometric pattern. It's a very easy bag to make with any 4in blocks – see the Block Library starting on page 116 for ideas.

You Will Need

Add seam allowances to all fabric and wadding sizes – see page 5

- Patchwork blocks from fabric scraps:
  four 4in square Canadian Gardens blocks
  four 4in square Fair and Square blocks

- Checked fabric pieces:
  four A 16in x 5in
  two B 16in x 4in

- Denim 6in x 16in for bag base

- Backing fabric two pieces 16in x 4in

- 2oz cotton wadding (batting)
  two pieces 16in x 4in

- Lining fabric pieces:
  two 16in x 14in
  two 16in x 4in
  one 6in x 16in for lining base

- 42in length of 1½in wide nylon
  webbing for straps

- Four 17in lengths of covered piping cord

- Sewing and quilting threads to tone
  with patchwork

Making the Patchwork

1 Begin by making four Canadian Gardens variation blocks and four Fair and Square blocks, using the diagram given in **Fig 1**, scaling each block up to 4in square. Each block is made from an assortment of strips, squares, Flying Geese blocks and triangle squares (see page 98). Sew two patchwork pieces of four blocks each, alternating the two block designs.

2 For each patchwork panel, using one piece of wadding (batting) and one piece of backing, make a quilt sandwich (see page 103) and then machine quilt each panel (see page 103), following the dashed lines in Fig 1. See page 103 for marking a quilting pattern.

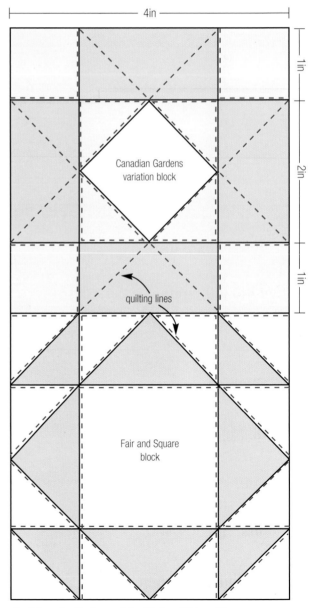

Fig 1 *Canadian Gardens variation block and Fair and Square block – scale each up to 4in square and make 4 of each block*

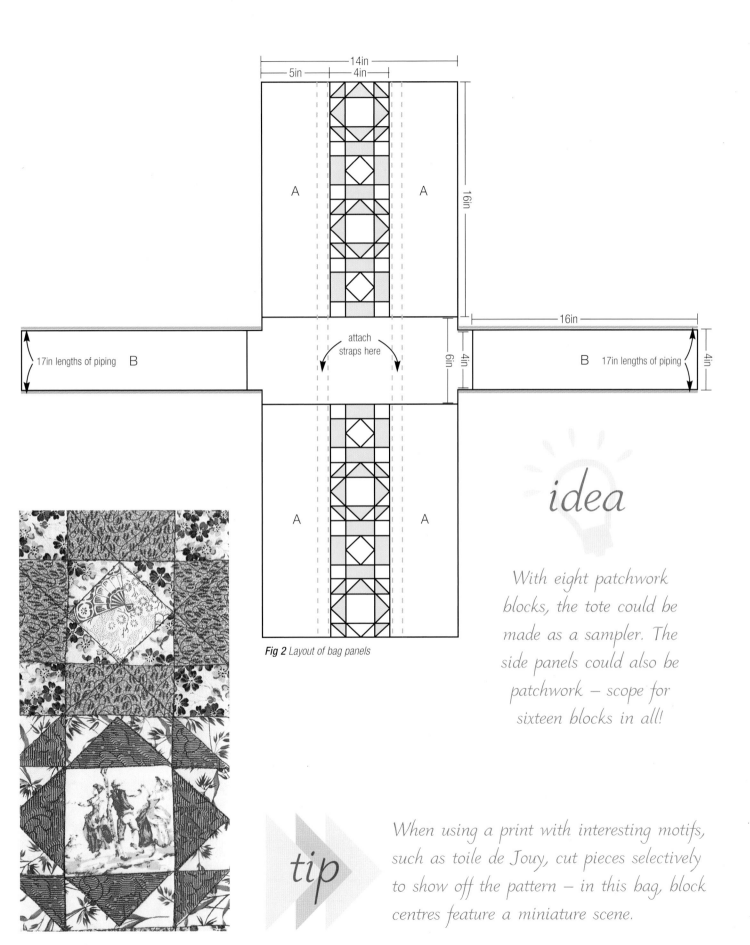

14in
5in
4in
16in
A
A
attach
straps here
17in lengths of piping B
16in
B 17in lengths of piping
4in
6in
4in

Fig 2 Layout of bag panels

idea

With eight patchwork
blocks, the tote could be
made as a sampler. The
side panels could also be
patchwork – scope for
sixteen blocks in all!

tip

When using a print with interesting motifs,
such as toile de Jouy, cut pieces selectively
to show off the pattern – in this bag, block
centres feature a miniature scene.

Constructing the Bag

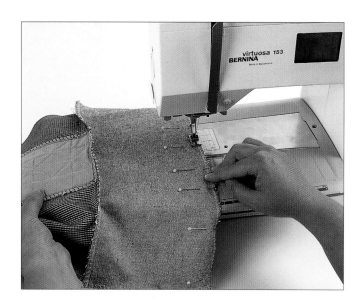

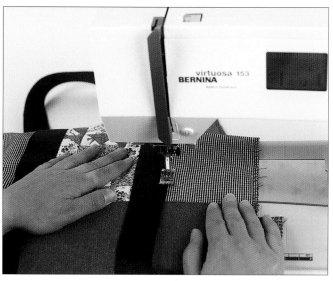

3 Using the checked fabric pieces and following the layout in **Fig 2**, machine sew one piece A to each side of each patchwork piece to make the bag panels. Shape the bag base by cutting a 1in square out of each corner. Sew the bag panels to the bag base to make the main bag panel and topstitch (see Tip).

4 **Attaching the straps:** Sew the webbing strap to the main bag panel, according to the positions of the dashed lines on Fig 2. The strap is sewn as a continuous loop, passing right under the bag base and up each side. Start and finish the raw ends of the strap just above the base section, overlapping the ends of the webbing. Oversew the raw end with machine zigzag and sew straight across the ends several times to secure. Machine sew along the long edge of the strap stopping 1½in from the top edge of the first bag panel, sew a figure of eight and sew back along the other edge of the strap, continuing up to the top edge of the other bag panel. Repeat the figure of eight and sew along the remaining edge (see straps page 110). Check that the strap loops are equal in length, pin the remaining part of the strap in place and repeat as above to sew the rest of the strap loop to the bag.

5 **Sewing side panels and piping:** Sew each side panel B to the base section of the main bag panel and topstitch. Prepare the piping by gently pulling the ends of the piping cord out from the folded piping fabric and trimming off 1in. This flattens the end of the piping making insertion into the seam easy. Pin and tack (baste) each piece of piping to the four seam edges of the main bag panel pieces. Note how the end of the piping is curved into the seam allowance. Pin the side panels to the main bag panel and machine sew the assembly seam using a zipper foot to sew close to the piping.

tip

Make the bag base extra strong by top stitching ⅛in away from the seam line, on the base side of the seam. The seam allowance should be pressed towards the base. Press and stitch side panels B away from the base.

Make your own piping with plain white piping cord (available in different thicknesses) and a bias cut strip of fabric (see bindings page 106). Try using striped or patterned fabric for an interesting effect.

idea

6 Making the lining: Make the bag lining the same way as the bag. Machine sew the main lining panels and side lining panels to the base lining. Machine sew the side panels to the main lining panels. When sewing the third end panel in place, leave a gap approximately 4in unsewn, for bagging out. To sew the lining into the bag, turn the bag right side out and with the lining turned wrong side out, place the bag inside the lining. Machine sew the lining to the bag along the long top edge of the bag sides only. Bag out and slipstitch the unsewn gap closed, then machine stitch all round, ⅛in from the edge.

Variation

Make the tote in a smaller size for a pretty shoulder bag. I used Victorian print fabric for simple piecing and appliquéd a hexagon flower made with English paper piecing (see page 101). The folded straps are decorated with broderie anglaise sewn to the webbing before the straps were assembled. Ready-made crochet embellishments and pretty mother-of-pearl buttons add to the nostalgic mood.

Double Bottle Bag

This double bottle bag, a different way to carry two bottles, takes advantage of the way cotton prints can stretch when used on the bias, fitting the bottles comfortably. I based this bag on a method of wrapping two bottles with a traditional Japanese *furoshiki* gift-wrapping cloth. Despite its complicated appearance, it is made from a flat, machine-pieced panel, which is then oversewn into a cylinder. The casual knotted handle is retied every time the bag is used, securing the bottles in place. The festive winter prints are enhanced by simple machine quilting in metallic threads, adding sparkle.

You Will Need

Add seam allowances to all fabric and wadding sizes – see page 5

- One patchwork panel 22in square from fabric scraps (random 2in strips and squares)

- One patchwork panel 22in square from two 10½in x 22in pieces and one 1in x 22in strip

- Four pieces of cotton lining fabric 11in x 22in

- Backing fabric two 22in squares of muslin or other loosely woven cotton

- 2oz soft polyester wadding (batting) 15in x 30in

- Sewing thread to tone with patchwork fabrics

- Gold metallic machine threads or similar hand embroidery threads

- Metallic machine needle

Making the Patchwork

1 Begin by making one patchwork panel from eleven strips, using the pattern given in **Fig 1** (see machine piecing, page 97). The finished width of each strip is 2in but the length of individual pieces is random. Cut various lengths 2½in wide, machine sew the ends together to make a long patchwork strip and then cut pieces from the completed strip. Make the second patchwork panel using the pattern given in **Fig 2**. Cut each square in half diagonally to make two triangles and arrange as shown in **Fig 3**, placing the triangles cut from the first panel in the middle of the long strip. Machine piece together. Trim off each end to make a point, as shown in the diagram. Repeat Fig 3 with backing fabric.

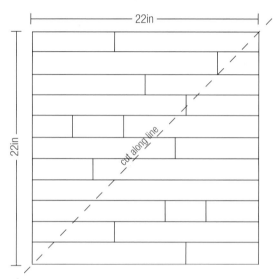

Fig 1 Patchwork panel from random 2in strips and squares – make 1 and cut in half diagonally

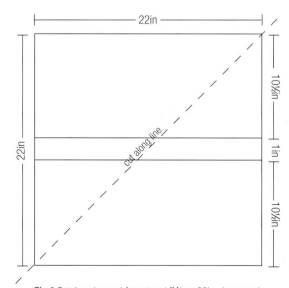

Fig 2 Patchwork panel from two 10½in x 22in pieces and one 1in x 22in strip – make 1 and cut in half diagonally

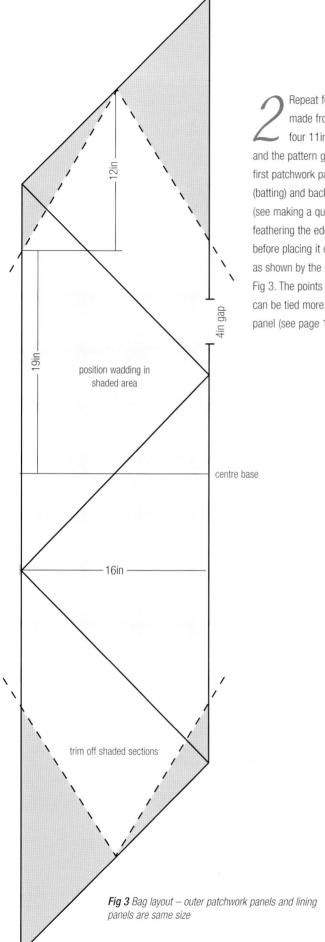

12in

4in gap

19in

position wadding in
shaded area

centre base

16in

trim off shaded sections

Fig 3 Bag layout – outer patchwork panels and lining panels are same size

2 Repeat for the bag lining panel, made from two squares using the four 11in x 22in fabric pieces and the pattern given in **Fig 4**. Using the first patchwork panel, the wadding (batting) and backing fabric, sandwich (see making a quilt sandwich page 103), feathering the edges of the wadding before placing it centrally in the sandwich as shown by the shaded central area in Fig 3. The points are not wadded so they can be tied more easily. Machine quilt the panel (see page 103).

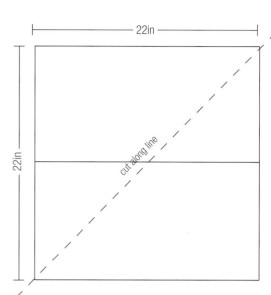

22in

22in

cut along line

Fig 4 Lining panel from two 11in x 22in pieces – make 2 and cut in half diagonally

tip

For simple but effective quilting, follow the grain of the fabric or large motifs in the pattern. Avoid quilting too much – the bag must be able to stretch slightly on the bias and dense quilting could prevent this. Try zigzag or wavy stitch patterns for extra flexibility.

Constructing the Bag

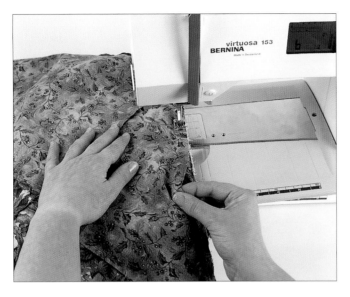

3 Pin the lining to the patchwork panel, right sides facing and machine sew together (using a stretch stitch if this is available on your machine). Sew a slightly rounded shape at the pointed ends, so the points are easier to turn out. Leave a gap approximately 4in unsewn, as shown in Fig 3.

4 Turn the bag right side out through the gap left in the stitching. Make sure the end points are well turned out and then slipstitch the gap closed.

5 Fold the bag in half lengthways down the centre with the lining on the outside. Starting at one end, oversew together to form a cylinder, stitching through the lining fabric only (this produces an attractive effect – a narrow strip of lining fabric visible along the seam line). Start and finish by oversewing in the opposite direction for approximately ½in.

6 Turn the bag cylinder right side out and machine sew across the bag at the halfway point to form the base.

Add a personalized touch to the double bottle bag with your own text messages on the patchwork strips. Use fabric dye pens or embroider the words by hand or machine.

idea

7 To use the double bottle bag, simply slip your bottles into the bag and tie the points together securely with a reef or square knot. The knot can then be used as a handle.

Variation

A rainbow colourway gives the bag a different mood. The fused appliqué details are very easy to do: following the manufacturer's instructions, iron the fusible material to the back of the fabric, cut out shapes and iron them on. I then edged the shapes with a machine embroidery stitch – it couldn't be easier. Rainbow-shaded thread was used for big stitch quilting (see page 105). I made a firmer, less flexible bag by using the straight grain of the fabric, rather than the diagonal, and wadding (batting) throughout. This bag fastens with two popper snaps, which children may prefer.

Quilter's Travel Bag

Tell the world you are a quilter on the move with this travel bag which is roomy but still small enough to fit in luggage racks and lockers easily. I travel a lot so I chose tough denim for the main fabric and used bits and pieces from my scrap bag to make the blocks. The theme is a country one, with Eight Point Stars and Flying Geese in checks and rustic prints. Some of my friends keep chickens, which inspired the star centres – each with a chicken 'portrait' cut selectively from a fat eighth of themed fabric. You could use other novelty prints for a different look. The external zip pocket keeps important items handy and the long strap can be removed when not required. (See picture on page 1 for other bags in this set specially for quilters.) Bon voyage!

You Will Need

Add seam allowances to all fabric and wadding sizes – see page 5

- Patchwork blocks from fabric scraps:
  ten 4in Eight Point Star blocks
  twenty-eight 1in x 2in Flying Geese units
  four 1in x 2in rectangles

- Medium-weight denim pieces:
  A 20in x 4¾in
  B 20in x 11½in
  C 20in x 5¾in
  D 20in x 1in
  E four 8in x 2in

- Backing fabric 20in x 31½in

- 2oz cotton wadding (batting) 20in x 31½in

- Main lining fabric 20in x 31½in

- Pocket lining fabric 20in x 13in

- 15in zip and 20in zip

- Nylon webbing 1½in wide:
  two 29in lengths (handles);
  two 3in lengths (D-ring tabs);
  one 44in length (shoulder strap)

- Two D-rings to fit webbing width

- Two swivel clips to fit webbing width

- Sewing and quilting threads to tone with patchwork

- Jeans topstitch thread

- Jeans machine needle

Making the Patchwork

1 Begin by making ten Eight Point Star blocks, using the pattern given in **Fig 1**. Each star is made from four small squares, one large square and four Flying Geese units (see page 98). Make two end panels by grouping four Eight Point Stars together as shown in **Fig 2**.

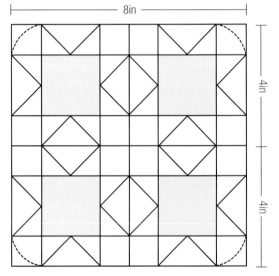

Fig 2 *Bag end panel of four Eight Point Star blocks – make 2*

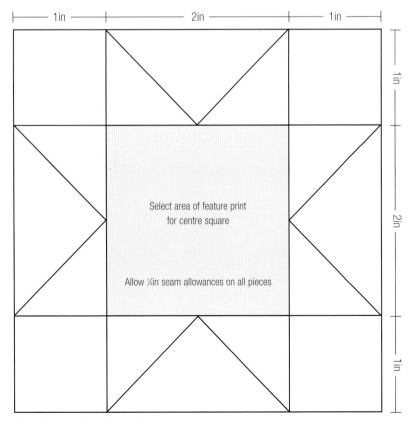

Select area of feature print for centre square

Allow ¼in seam allowances on all pieces

Fig 1 *Eight Point Star block pattern (actual size)*

2 Piece four Flying Geese units – these are made up of seven Flying Geese plus one rectangle (which will be hidden by the straps). Use **Fig 3** and follow the instructions on page 98.

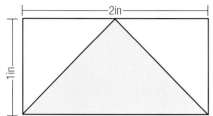

Fig 3 Flying Geese block pattern (actual size)

3 Using the Flying Geese units, the single Eight Point Stars and the denim pieces E, assemble the main bag panel, following **Fig 4**. Use ¼in seam allowances around all pieces and ½in seams on each side of the zip openings.

4 Machine sew two 29in nylon webbing handles to the bag (see attaching straps page 110), according to the positions on Fig 4. With denim pieces B, C and D, continue assembling the main bag panel. Keep piece A separate – the pocket zip will be sewn between pieces A and D later.

5 Cut wadding (batting) and backing fabric pieces to fit the main bag panel (keeping the remaining pieces for piece A). Using the wadding and backing fabric, make a quilt sandwich (see page 103) and machine quilt the panel: quilt in the ditch around the blocks. Use jeans topstitch thread to quilt the denim (see machine quilting page 103). Use remaining pieces of wadding (batting) and backing fabric to sandwich and quilt piece A with jeans topstitch thread.

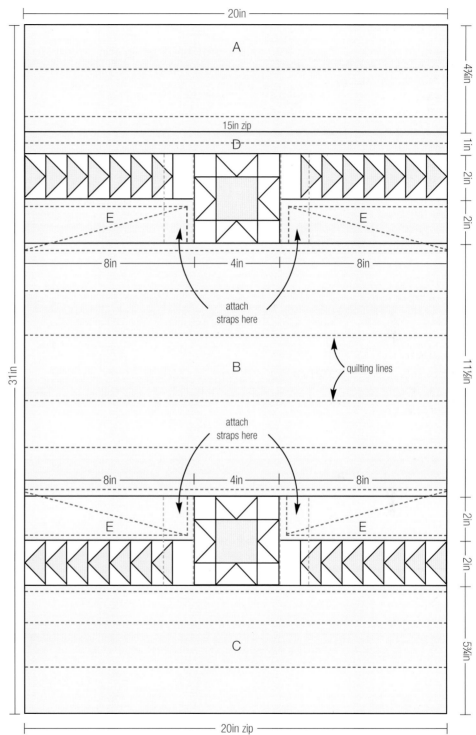

Fig 4 Main bag panel of patchwork and denim pieces – make 1

Constructing the Bag

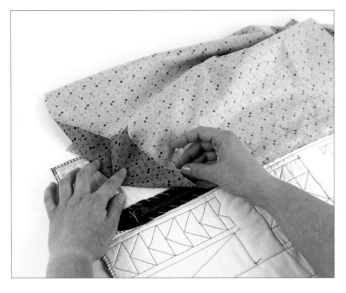

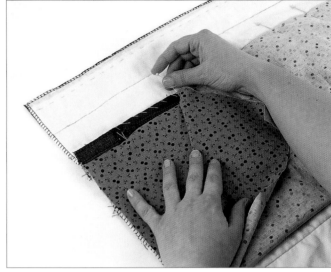

6 **Inserting the pocket zip and lining:** With right sides together, machine sew pieces A and D together 2½in at each end. Tack (baste) the zip opening closed. Tack the 15in zip in place between piece A and D (see inserting a zip invisibly page 108). Pin the pocket lining to the back of the zip as shown and tack (baste) in place. From the right side of the bag, machine sew the zip and pocket lining.

7 Fold up the pocket fabric, pin it over the side of the zip then tack (baste) in place. From the right side of the bag, machine sew the zip and pocket lining in place.

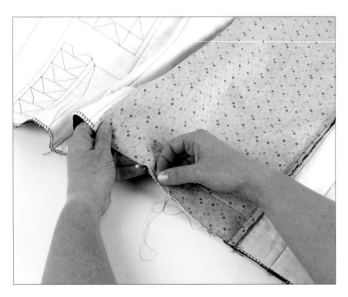

8 Tack (baste) the sides of the pocket lining to the sides of the bag panel. The raw edge of the pocket lining will be caught in the bag assembly seam when the end panels are sewn on later.

9 **Inserting the main zip and lining:** Sew the 20in zip into the top opening of the bag (see page 107). Fold a 3in length of webbing over a D-ring and machine sew in place (see attaching straps and D-rings page 110). Tack (baste) the D-ring tab to each end of the zip (see photo with step 11). The tab will be caught in the bag assembly seam. Repeat this with the other D-ring and tack (baste) it at the other end of the zip.

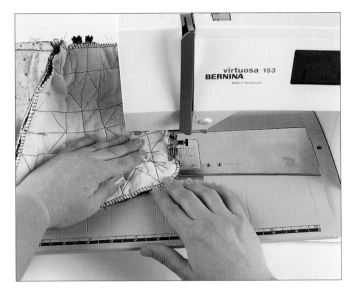

10 **Adding the end panels:** With right sides together, centre one of the patchwork end panels, aligning the midpoint of the bag side sections, base and top, with the midpoint of the panel. Pin in place and machine sew the assembly seam, taking care to ease the main bag panel around the curved corners. Repeat with the other end panel.

11 Using the 44in length of nylon webbing, make a long strap with a clip at each end (see making straps page 109). Alternatively, sew the strap directly to the D-rings.

tip *Allow ½in of tab to be caught in the bag assembly seam, to allow for the webbing fraying slightly.*

12 Using the main lining fabric, make the lining following the basic bag assembly instructions. Turn the lining right side out and turn the bag wrong side out. Place the bag inside the lining and slipstitch the lining to the back of the zip strip.

idea

For a simpler version of the bag, leave out the external zip pocket. Replace pieces A and D with a second piece C and leave out steps 6 – 8. Or add a patch pocket, as described on page 80.

Victorian Circle Bag

My first venture into patchwork (in common with many quilters) involved English paper piecing hexagons by hand. English paper piecing is more time consuming than machine piecing but, for patterns like the hexagon flower featured in this bag, can be worthwhile and produces accurate results. Above all, it is portable and I was able to stitch this bag in spare moments! I combined small scraps of reproduction Victorian prints and my love of antique quilts in the design. Paper pieced flowers were made from hexagons and diamonds, appliquéd to the side panels and then hand quilted. The Victorians didn't have zips but, as a concession to modern living, there is a zip in the bag gusset. The strap is attached with D-rings in an antique brass finish, matching the zip.

You Will Need

Add seam allowances to all fabric and wadding sizes – see page 5

- Patchwork panels from fabric scraps:
  two 8in diameter fabric circles
  two hexagon and diamond appliqué panels
  in assorted printed fabrics

- Fifteen 1in x 1in squares for patchwork gusset

- Two pieces fabric ½in x 10in for zip strip

- Backing fabric two 8½in diameter circles

and one strip 1in x 15in

- 2oz cotton wadding (batting):
  two 8in diameter circles;
  1in x 47in for strap;
  1in x 15in for gusset

- Fabric for strap 2⅛in x 50in

- Strap attachments: two leaf shapes in
  print fabric and two pieces of cotton
  tape the same length

- Lining fabric pieces:
  two 8in diameter circles
  one 15in x 1in for gusset
  two 10in x 1in for behind zip

- 8in zip

- Two antique brass-finish D-rings to fit 1in strap

- Sewing and quilting threads to tone
  with patchwork

Making the Patchwork

1 Begin by making two patchwork panels using **Fig 1** to cut the templates (for each panel: seven hexagons, six half hexagons and eighteen diamonds). Hand sew the panels using English paper piecing (see page 101). Use ¼in seam allowances around all fabric pieces.

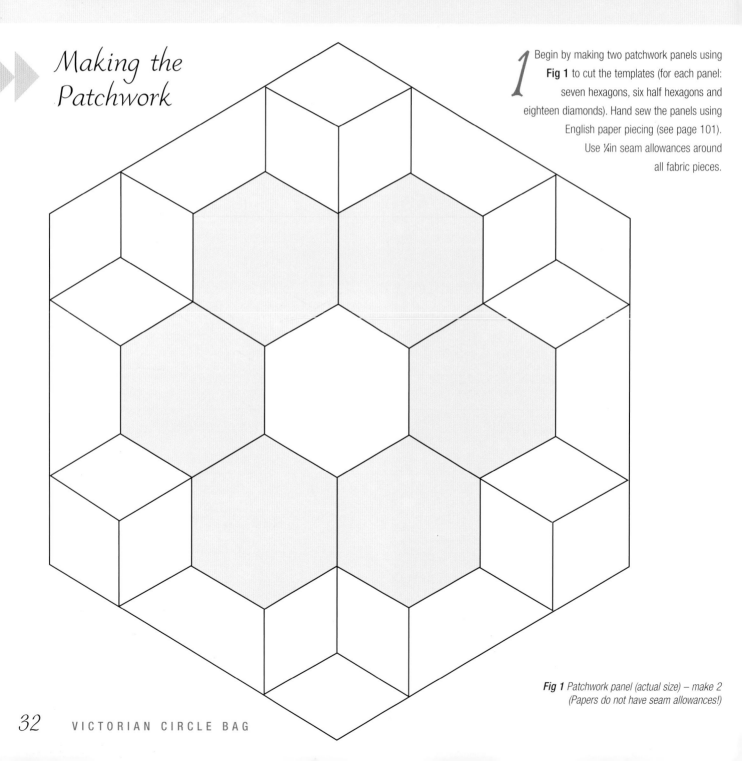

*Fig 1 Patchwork panel (actual size) – make 2
(Papers do not have seam allowances!)*

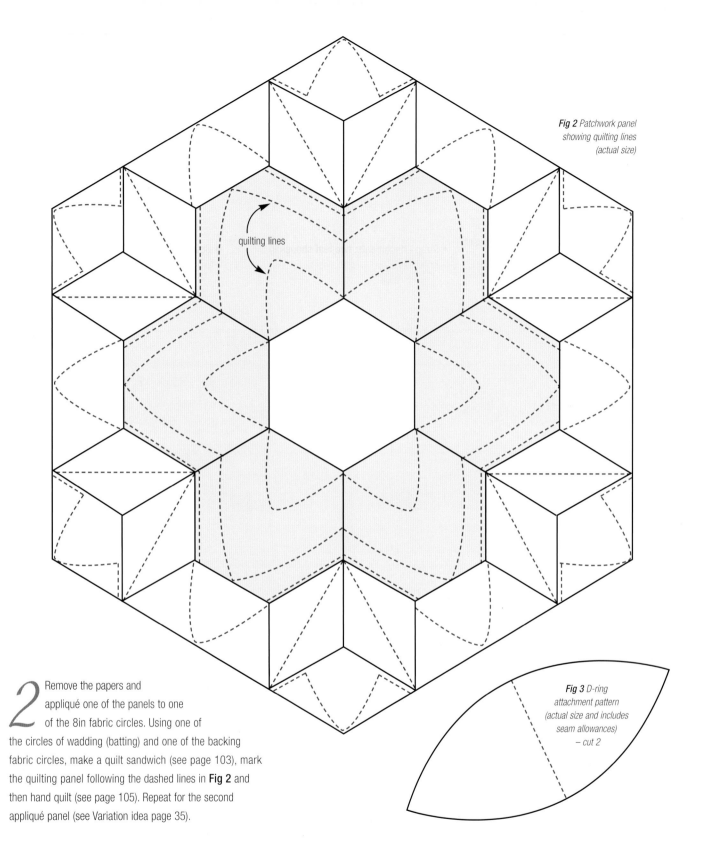

Fig 2 Patchwork panel
showing quilting lines
(actual size)

quilting lines

2 Remove the papers and
   appliqué one of the panels to one
   of the 8in fabric circles. Using one of
the circles of wadding (batting) and one of the backing
fabric circles, make a quilt sandwich (see page 103), mark
the quilting panel following the dashed lines in **Fig 2** and
then hand quilt (see page 105). Repeat for the second
appliqué panel (see Variation idea page 35).

Fig 3 D-ring
attachment pattern
(actual size and includes
seam allowances)
– cut 2

3 Using the fifteen 1in
   squares (1½in squares
   including seam allowances),
assemble the patchwork strip
gusset. Sandwich and quilt with two
parallel lines running the length of
the strip.

Constructing the Bag

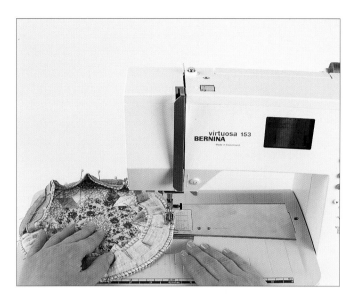

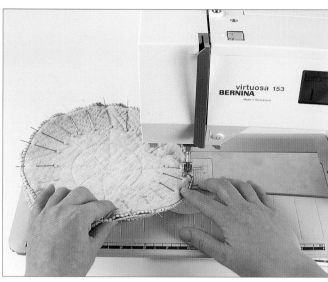

4 Assemble the zip gusset without any quilting, using a ⅛in seam allowance for the zip edge (see inserting a zip invisibly page 108). Sew gusset ends to the ends of the zip gusset to make a loop. Pin the completed gusset to the bag side panel and machine sew in place.

5 Pin the second bag panel to the gusset and machine sew in place (see Tip below).

tip Sewing the gusset to the side panel is shown both ways, i.e., with the bag gusset pinned to the side panel and with the side panel pinned to the gusset. Assemble your bag whichever way you find easiest.

6 Using the 2½in x 50in piece of fabric, make a folded strap (see straps page 109) and attach it to the D-rings. Use **Fig 3** to cut two leaf shapes from the same fabric used for the strap (seam allowances are already included). Tack (baste) cotton tape strip to the wrong side of each leaf for added strength and trim to shape. Turn under ¼in all round the leaf shapes and herringbone stitch in place (see page 113). Fold the leaf over the straight part of the D-ring and sew in place. Attach the D-rings and strap to the bag, at either end of the patchwork gusset, with leaf attachments. Now pin the leaf to the gusset on either side of the zip and backstitch in place, then slipstitch the edges down.

7 Make the lining by first folding over ½in seam allowance along one edge of each 10½in x 1in lining fabric. Butt the folded edges together and sew the ends to the gusset lining. Sew the completed gusset lining loop to the lining sides, as in steps 4 and 5. Turn the bag lining right side out. Turn the bag wrong side out and place inside the lining. Slipstitch the lining to the back of the zip and then turn the bag right side out.

idea   Instead of making a bag with two sides the same, make it with two different panels. This picture shows the reverse of the bag on page 30 – a patchwork star made with a foundation piecing technique (see page 99). It contrasts with the hexagon panel while providing a larger central area to feature a reproduction print. The star was easy to make in two halves, with the circle centre appliquéd last.

Long Workbag

I needed a long workbag for my needlepoint (tapestry) frame but realised how useful it would be for leisure as well. This version would be great for lazy days on the beach as it's long enough for rolled beach mats and towels. Wooden dowels inserted in slots in the bag top keep the shape rigid and can easily be removed for washing. The straps are sewn into the bag seams so they can't come undone, and I used a decorative machine stitch to sew the straps to the side panels. The lining is simply sewn in and bagged out. The striped canvas fabric was originally bought to cover a deck chair! I had fun making the Sailing Ship and Beach Hut blocks in sun-bleached shades, with combined machine and hand quilting. Ready-made cord loop-and-ball fasteners add the finishing touch.

You Will Need

Add seam allowances to all fabric and wadding sizes – see page 5

- Patchwork blocks from fabric scraps:
  one 8in square Sailing Ship block
  one 8in square Beach Hut block

- Striped canvas pieces:
  A 24in x 10in
  B four 8in squares
  C two 24in x 1in
  D two 8in squares
  two 47in x 1½in for straps

- Backing fabric two 8in squares

- 2oz cotton wadding (batting) two 8in squares

- Lining fabric:
  one 24in x 27½in
  Two 8in squares

- Two 23in wooden dowels ⅜in diameter

- Two 47in x 1in pieces of cotton webbing
  for straps

- Two brass popper fasteners (with punch tools)

- Two ready-made loop-and-ball fasteners

- Sewing and quilting threads to tone with patchwork fabrics

- Shaded medium hand-sewing thread

Making the Patchwork

1 Begin by making one Sailing Ship block and one Beach Hut block, using the diagrams given in **Fig 1** and **Fig 2** (scaled up to 8in squares). Each block is made from an assortment of strips, squares, Flying Geese blocks and triangle squares (see page 98).

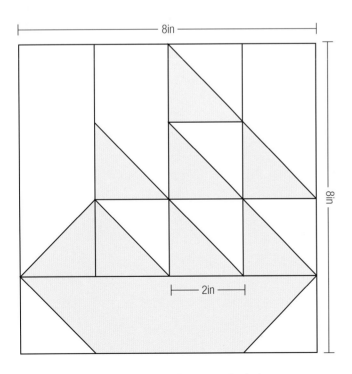

Fig 1 Sailing Ship block – scale up to 8in square and make 1

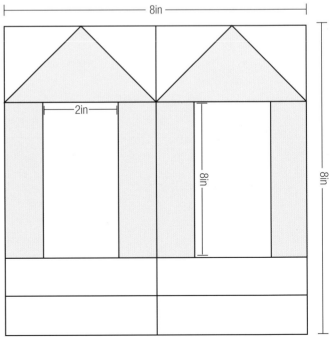

Fig 2 Beach Hut block – scale up to 8in square and make 1

2 For each block, use a piece of wadding (batting) and backing, make a quilt sandwich (see page 103) and machine quilt, in the ditch, around the ship, sails, beach huts and hut doors. Using shaded thread, hand quilt the sky in big stitch.

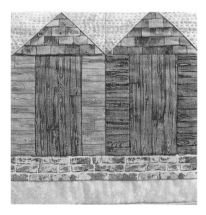

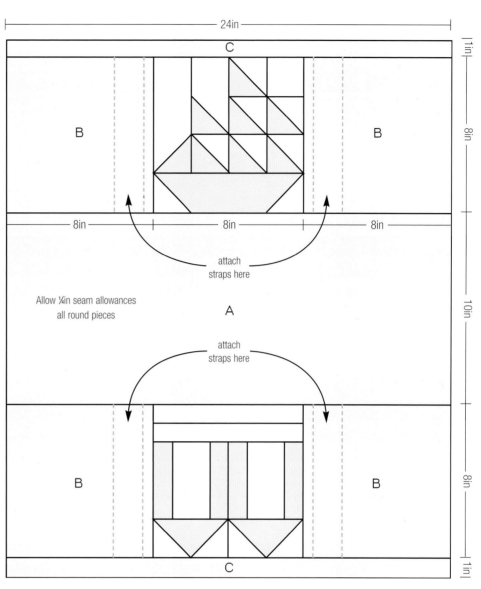

Fig 3 *Main bag panel – make 1*

Constructing the Bag

3 Using the canvas pieces and following **Fig 3**, machine sew one piece B to each side of each patchwork block to make side panels. Machine sew one piece C to the top of each side panel. Machine sew canvas piece A to the bag side panels.

tip

Make the main bag panel extra strong by top stitching ⅛in away from the seam line, on the pressed seam allowance side.

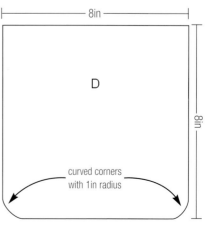

Fig 4 *End panel – make 2*

Constructing the Bag

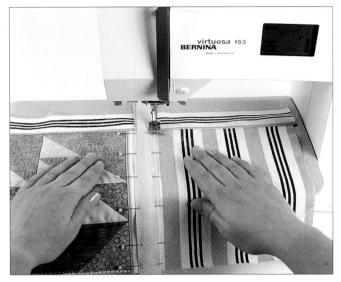

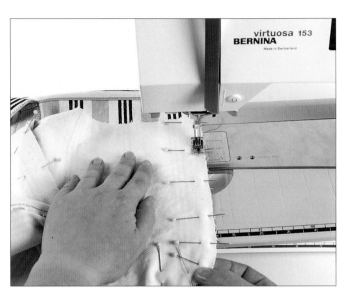

4   Make folded straps using the two 47in x 1¼in canvas pieces and the cotton webbing (see straps, page 109) and sew to the side panels, according to the positions of the dashed lines on **Fig 3**. The ends of the straps will be caught in the bag assembly seam but allow ½in of each strap in this seam in case the webbing frays slightly.

5   Trim the two bottom corners of each canvas piece D to make curved corners with a radius of 1in (**Fig 4**). Trim the two 8in squares of lining fabric the same way. Fold each piece D in half vertically and mark the centre of the bottom edge. Fold the main bag panel in half along the base section and mark with a pin at each end of the fold. With right sides together, pin each piece D to the main bag panel, matching up centre pins. Machine sew, starting and stopping ¼in from the end of the seam, easing the main bag panel around the corner curves. Note: piece D is shorter than the main bag panel.

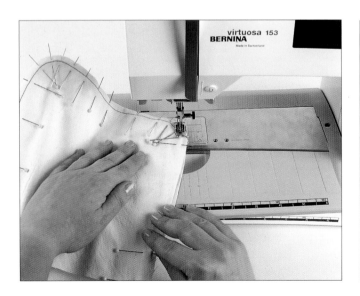

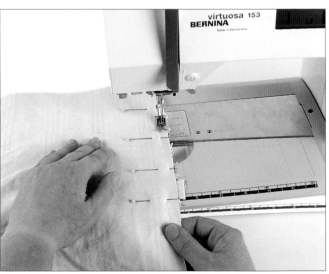

6   **Making the lining:** Make the bag lining the same way as the bag. Machine sew the end lining panels to the main lining panel. When sewing the second end panel in place, leave a gap approximately 4in unsewn for bagging out.

7   To sew the lining into the bag, turn the bag right side out. With the lining turned wrong side out, place the bag inside the lining. Machine sew the lining to the bag along the long top edge of bag sides only.

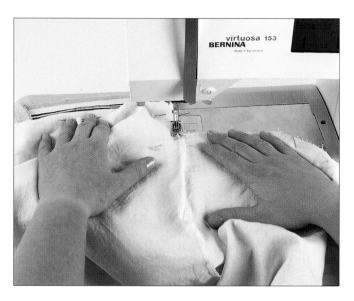

8 Line up the bag ends with the lining ends and continue machine sewing the edge of the lining to the edge of the bag. As the lining is slightly shorter than the bag sides, the outer bag fabric will overlap slightly towards the inside along the long top edges. Leave a ½in unsewn gap at each end of the long top edge, to make the dowel pocket.

9 Clip into corners where the end panels are sewn into the bag, being careful not to cut the stitching. Bag out, by turning the bag right side out through the gap left in the lining. Make sure corners are fully turned out.

10 Machine sew a ½in wide channel along the top of the bag on both sides for the dowels, leaving the channel ends open. Top stitch around the ends of the bag.

11 **Adding fasteners:** In order that the bag ends can be snapped closed securely, add a popper fastener to each end panel of the bag, following the manufacturer's instructions. To make a neatly fastened fold, insert the poppers from the inside of the bag. Alternatively, use press-stud fasteners, sewn in place.

12 Remove any roughness from the lengths of dowel with glass paper and then slip the dowels into the channels along the top of the bag. The dowels should be a good snug fit. Leave the channel ends open so the dowels can be removed if you need to wash the bag. To finish, hand sew loop-and-ball fasteners to the top of the bag.

Variation

I used a country theme for a second long workbag. The bag closes with an open-end zip (the kind used for jackets) so it can be opened wide. Without the dowels, this bag risked being too soft and shapeless, so I added stiff pelmet interfacing to the base, between the wadding (batting) and the backing in the quilt sandwich. It worked!

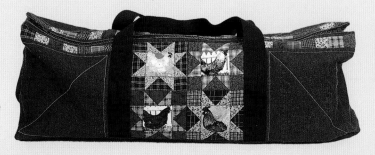

Quilter's Briefcase

Following accidental damage to my cutting mat, I designed this briefcase to keep all my quilting equipment safe. There are plenty of pockets – on the inside for my small mat and rulers, and on the outside for magazines and folders. It's just as popular with non-quilters! The external pocket tops are bound with a double straight binding for strength while the internal pocket top is reinforced with cotton tape. The main bag assembly seam is on the outside and covered with a double bias binding. I used compressed 6oz wadding (batting) for a firm, flat bag and 1¼in wide nylon webbing for durable straps. The view from my workroom window inspired the foundation-pieced side panels. Try using the colours of your local landscape for a harmonious scheme. As an alternative to foundation piecing, the landscape could be appliquéd.

You Will Need

Add seam allowances to all fabric and wadding
sizes – see page 5

- Two foundation-pieced patchwork panels
  16in x 9in from assorted fat eighths and strips

- One patchwork base 16in x 6in from
  assorted strips

- Two pieces of foundation stabilizer 17in x 10in

- Two fabric pieces 16in x 11¾in for external
  pocket panels

- External pocket lining 16in x 23½in

- Fabric pieces for zip gusset:
  two 40in x 1¾in
  two 2in square

- Bias strip 2in x 96in to match zip gusset

- Backing fabric pieces:
  one 16in x 23½in
  two 16in x 11¾in

- 6oz compressed polyester wadding (batting):
  one 16in x 23½in
  two 16in x 11¾in

- Main lining fabric 16in x 30in

- Internal pocket fabric (to match lining)
  16in x 11in

- Cotton tape 1in x 16½in

- 40in zip (single- or double-pull)

- Two lengths nylon webbing 1¼in x 34½in

- Sewing and quilting threads to tone with
  patchwork fabrics

Making the Patchwork

1 Begin by making two foundation-pieced panels (see foundation
piecing page 99) – these will form the external pockets. Use **Fig 1**
and the photograph to help you draw your foundation pattern,
using straight lines to make the landscape. Use some of the same fabric
for the external pocket panel and the sky section in your patchwork, to
continue the cloud effect. Make the patchwork strip base from sixteen
strips, 1in x 6in, including some landscape fabrics. Following **Fig 1**,
machine sew the foundation-pieced panels to the patchwork strip base
to make the main bag panel.

2 With the 16in x 23½in piece of wadding (batting) and the same
size backing fabric, make a quilt sandwich (see page 103) and
quilt the main bag panel, using continuous machine quilting in the
ditch and zigzag quilting to enhance the patchwork, starting and finishing at
the edges. Place the wrong side of the external pocket lining to the wrong
side of the main bag panel and machine sew around the edges. Machine
sew straight binding to the pocket tops and finish by hand sewing (see
making bindings page 106).

3 With one of the 16in x 11¾in pieces of wadding (batting) and the
same size backing fabric, sandwich and quilt one of the external
pocket pieces. Machine quilt in zigzags and straight lines from side
to side. Repeat for the other external pocket piece. Trim top corners to make
curves with a 3in radius.

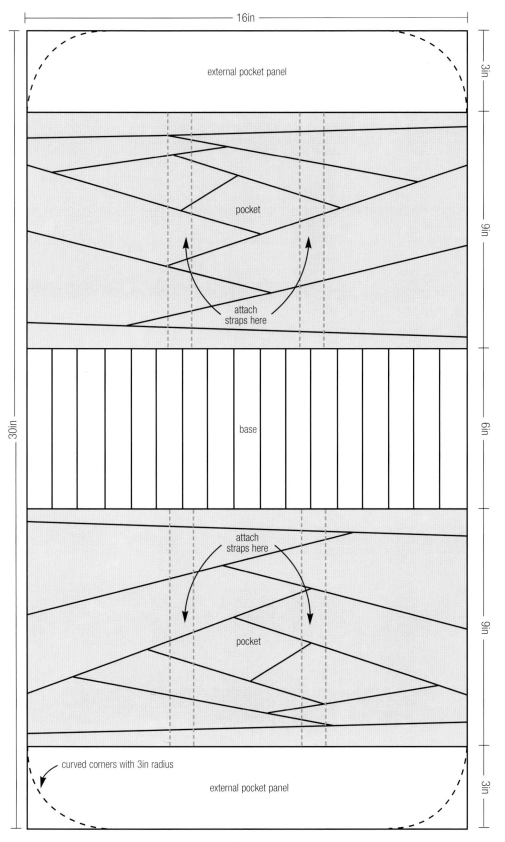

Fig 1 *Main bag panel – make 1*

Add ¼in seam allowance round all pieces

tip

Stitch around the completed foundation piecing ⅛in from the edge to stabilize the bias edges before removing the stabilizer (if using a paper or tear-off type) just before layering and quilting.

Constructing the Bag

4 Using the nylon webbing, add straps to the back of the main bag panel, machine sewing them in place just below the binding at the top, according to the positions of the dashed lines on Fig 1 (see attaching straps page 110). Leave the rest of the straps unsewn. The webbing will be caught later in the external pocket base seam.

idea

If you wish, add a hook-and-loop tape closure to the external pockets (see Zipover Rucksack). Sew the tape to the inside top edge of the main bag panel and on the corresponding place on the external pocket panel.

5 **Attaching the external pockets:** Trim the two top corners of both external pocket panels to make curved corners each with a radius of 2in. These external pocket panels will be machine sewn to the main bag panel along the landscape panel/base panel seams. Mark the ends of the seam line position on the back of the main bag panel, i.e. on the lining. (Note: the straps have been omitted in the photograph for clarity.)

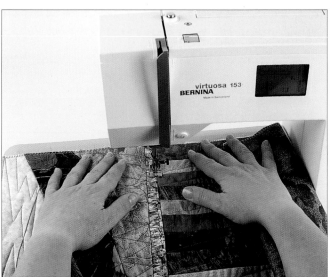

6 Each external pocket panel should overlap the base landscape panel seam line by ¼in. Mark a second line to help with positioning the edge of each external pocket panel, allowing for this overlap. Pin each external pocket panel to the back of the main bag panel and tack (baste).

7 From the right side of the main bag panel, machine sew the external pocket panels in place, stitching in the ditch along the base landscape panel seam line to conceal the stitches. The strap ends are caught in this seam between the external pocket panels and main bag panel.

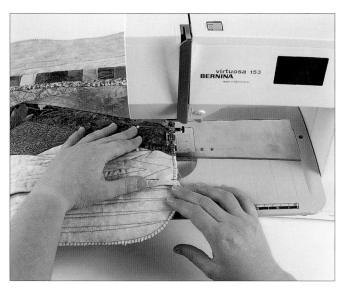

8 Machine sew the external pocket panels to the sides of the main bag panel. The edges of the pocket panels will be caught in the bag assembly seam when the zip strip is attached.

9 **Making the lining with pocket:** To make the lining with an internal pocket, start by folding over the top edge of the pocket fabric piece ¼in towards the wrong side. Machine sew both edges of 1in wide cotton tape reinforcement to the wrong side of the pocket along the top edge to hide the raw edge. Now draw a line across the lining fabric 12in from the top edge and, with right sides facing, pin the base of the pocket in place along this line. Machine sew the base of the pocket to the lining, flip the pocket up and sew the pocket sides in place. The edges of the pocket will be caught in the bag assembly seam when the zip is attached.

Cotton tape prevents the top of the pocket stretching in use. Alternatively, make a decorative reinforcement on the outside edge of the pocket with ribbon or braid.

10 Using the bias cut strip, make double bias binding (see making bindings page 106). Pin and tack (baste) the binding around the outside edge of the bag, being careful not to stretch the binding. The zip gusset, binding and pockets are sewn in place in one step with the main bag assembly seam. Take care with tacking (basting) to secure all the layers in place accurately before machine sewing the next step.

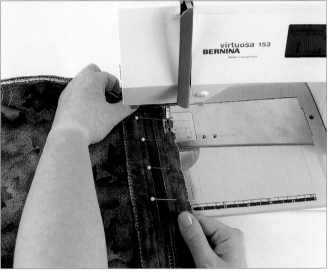

11 **Making the zip gusset:** Using the zip, two pieces of fabric 40in x 1¾in and two pieces 2in square, make the zip gusset (see page 107). Check the length of the finished gusset against the edge of the main panel and trim ends as necessary. Fold the main bag panel in half along the base section and mark the fold with a pin at both ends. With wrong sides together, pin the middle of the gusset ends to the edge of the main bag panel, matching up the pins. Continue to pin the ends of the gusset to the edge of the main bag panel. Machine sew, starting and stopping ¼in from the end of the seam to allow for turning the corner.

12 Clip the main bag panel ⅛in where it will turn the corner of the zip gusset, ¼in from the seam end – sufficient to turn the corner without weakening the bag. Pin the long sides of the zip gusset to the edge of the main bag panel and machine sew along both sides, stopping before the corner curve. Repeat for the other side. Continue pinning and sewing, easing the zip gusset around the curve, clipping ⅛in into the gusset at corners as necessary.

tip With a double-pull zip you can open the briefcase from the top outwards in both directions, thus opening the top without opening the side first.

13 When the machine stitching is complete, finish the bag by folding the bias binding over and slipstitching it in place all around the bag.

Variation

Made to co-ordinate with the Quilter's Travel Bag (see page 24 and also photograph on page 1), this country version replaces the external open pockets with a zip pocket on the outside. Cotton wadding (batting) and seams on the inside make a softer bag. I added two pockets on the inside and embroidered the pocket tops on the machine. To make the briefcase more capacious, the zip gusset, with a concealed zip, was widened and the outer panel dimensions lengthened slightly to fit.

Small Workbag

When my quilting friend Reiko visited the UK, she carried her sewing essentials in a neat little bag which inspired me to design my own version. This workbag is similar to the Quilter's Briefcase on page 42 but the seams are on the inside. The smaller size looks good made completely in patchwork. I machine pieced Delectable Mountains to complement the retro-print cottons and continued the 1930s theme with machine quilting echoing Art Deco patterns. The lining is fitted with pockets and elastic loops for scissors, rulers, pencils, thread and so on, and you can adapt these features to suit your needs. With this small workbag, you can have your hand sewing essentials conveniently packed and ready to go, whenever you want!

You Will Need

Add seam allowances to all fabric and wadding sizes – see page 5

- One patchwork panel 8in x 14in:
  two Delectable Mountain blocks 8in x 6in
  one base strip 8in x 1½in

- Two pieces of fabric 20in x 1½in for zip gusset

- Backing fabric 8in x 14in

- 6oz compressed polyester wadding (batting) 8in x 14in

- Lining fabric pieces:
  one 8in x 14in
  two 20in x 1½in for zip gusset
  oddments of extra fabric for inner pockets

- Oddments of cotton tape, elastic, buttons

- 20in zip

- Sewing and quilting threads to tone with patchwork fabrics

Making the Patchwork

1 Begin by making the two Delectable Mountain blocks, finished size 8in x 6in. For each block, start with one 6⅞in square each of light and dark print fabric (size includes seam allowances) and make two triangle squares (see page 98). Cut two 4in squares from the same fabric (size includes seam allowance) for each block and use to sew a smaller triangle to the dark half of each triangle square, as if sewing half a Flying Geese unit (see page 98). Lay out the two patchwork squares as shown in **Fig 1a**, cut each piece into four 1¼in strips and one ½in strip (discard the ½in strip). Rearrange and sew the strips together using the pattern in **Fig 1b**. Sew the two halves of the Delectable Mountain block together. Repeat for the second block.

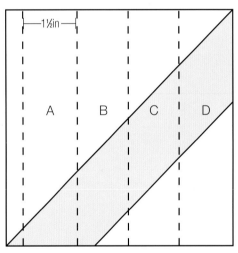
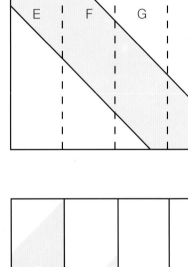

Fig 1a Patchwork pieces – cut along dotted lines and make 2

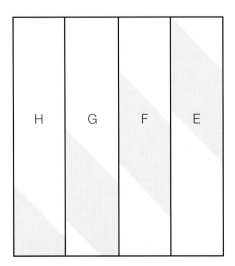
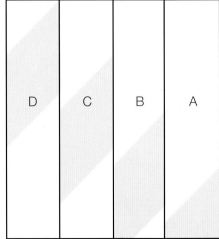

Fig 1b Rearrange strips in order shown to form Delectable Mountains block

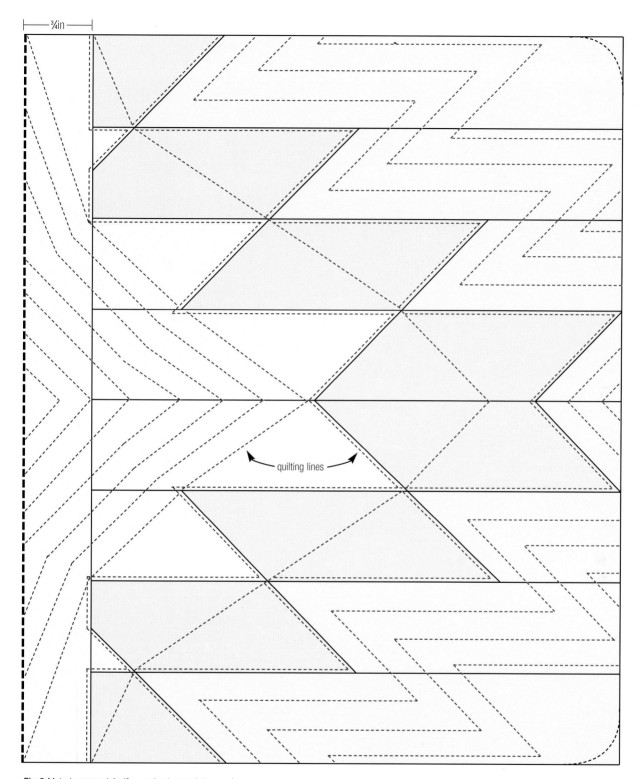

¾in

quilting lines

Fig 2 Main bag panel (half) – make 1 complete panel

2 Sew one Delectable Mountain block to each side of the 8in x 1½in
base strip using the pattern given in **Fig 2**. Trim the corners to
curves with a radius of 1in. Using the wadding (batting) and
backing fabric,make a quilt sandwich (see page 103), and quilt. Mark
quilting lines, following the dashed lines in **Fig 2**, and machine quilt
starting and finishing at the edge (see page 103).

Constructing the Bag

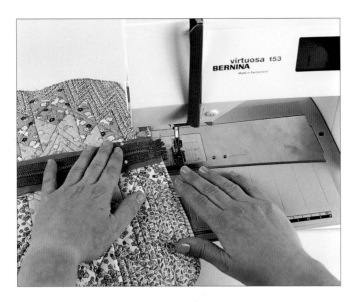

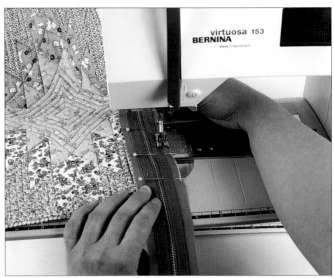

3 **Making the zip gusset:** Using the zip and two pieces of fabric 20in x 1½in, make the zip gusset (see inserting a visible zip page 107). Fold the main bag panel in half along the base section right sides together and mark the fold with a pin at each end. Pin the middle of the zip gusset ends to the edge of the main bag panel, matching up the pins. Continue to pin the ends of the zip gusset to the edge of the main bag panel. Machine sew, starting and stopping ¼in from the end of the seam to allow for turning the corner.

4 Clip the edge of the main bag panel ⅛in where it will turn the corner of the zip gusset, ¼in from the end of the seam. This will be sufficient to turn the corner without weakening the bag. Pin the long sides of the zip gusset to the edge of the bag and machine sew along each side, stopping before the corner curve. Repeat for the other side of bag. Continue pinning and sewing, easing the zip gusset around the curve, clipping ⅛in into the edge of the zip gusset at corners as necessary.

idea *Jazz up a plain zip with a decorative metal charm, attaching it to the zip pull with a jump ring. Alternatively, make and attach a miniature tassel.*

5 **Making the lining:** Assemble the lining with pockets, loops and so on to store your sewing equipment (see adding extra pockets page 110). Check the size of your scissors, rulers and cutters and make loops and pockets to fit. Embellish the fabric edges with decorative machine stitching as I have done if you wish. Make a thread spool holder with a loop of elastic and a button in the bottom of the bag – the raw ends of the elastic will be caught in the lining seam. Sew strips of cotton tape over the ends of the elastic loops to neaten and hide any raw edges that will not be caught in the lining seam.

Finish making the lining following the bag construction instructions, using the two pieces of 20in x 1½in lining fabric instead of the zip gusset. Place the bag wrong side out and slipstitch the lining to the back of the zip gusset. Then slipstitch the lining to the bag along the lining seam with small running stitches, taking care not to go through to the outside of the bag. This will keep the lining in place when your workbag is fully packed.

Variation

This country version was made with a single Eight Point Star block on one side and some scrap strips only on the other side, left over from making the Quilter's Travel Bag. I added big stitch quilting (see page 105) with shaded perlé cotton for a more rustic look, after machine quilting in the ditch around the star block. The thread holder and elastic loops were omitted in favour of a simple lining with a pocket for a notebook (made the same way as the Quilter's Briefcase internal pocket). You could add extra zipped pockets for pens and pencils (see inserting the pocket zip, Quilter's Travel Bag, page 28).

Fan Purse

Only two fabrics are needed to make this unusual purse – simple foundation piecing with a large scale Oriental print breaks up the pattern and gives the illusion of a folded paper fan. It's perfect for a special evening out and the right size for a few essentials. I enhanced the patchwork with machine quilting in metallic thread to emphasize the fan effect. Two 'fans' are joined to make a circle, which is then quilted, bound and folded. As the purse is small, the zip fastener was sewn in by hand.

You Will Need

Add seam allowances to all fabric and wadding
sizes – see page 5

- Two semicircular foundation-pieced
  patchwork panels 9in x 4½in:
  sixteen 2in x 3in for fan 'papers'
  two 3in semicircles for appliqué
  two pieces of foundation stabilizer
  10in x 5½in

- Backing fabric 9in diameter circle

- 2oz cotton wadding (batting) 9in
  diameter circle

- Lining fabric 9in diameter circle

- One 8in zip

- Bias cut fabric strip 2in x 30in
  to match semicircles

- Sewing and quilting threads
  to tone with patchwork

- Plain and shaded metallic machine
  embroidery threads

- Metallic machine needle

Making the Patchwork

1 Begin by making two foundation-
pieced fans, finished size 9in x 4½in.
For each block, trace the pattern
shown in **Fig 1** on to a stabilizer such as
greaseproof paper (wax paper). Foundation
piece the 'folds' of the fan (see foundation
piecing on paper page 100). Hand appliqué
(see page 102) a semicircle of plainer
fabric to the centre of each fan and
straight machine stitch around the whole
block, ⅛in from the edge, before removing
the stabilizer paper. Sew the two fans
together to make the circular bag panel.

2 Using the wadding (batting) and
backing fabric, make a quilt
sandwich (see page 103), and
machine quilt (see page 103). Mark quilting
lines for the fan 'sticks' following the
dashed lines in **Fig 1**, and machine quilt in
metallic thread. Use plain gold metallic
thread in straight stitch for the fan's 'folds'
and a variegated gold and copper thread in
a narrow zigzag for the 'sticks'.

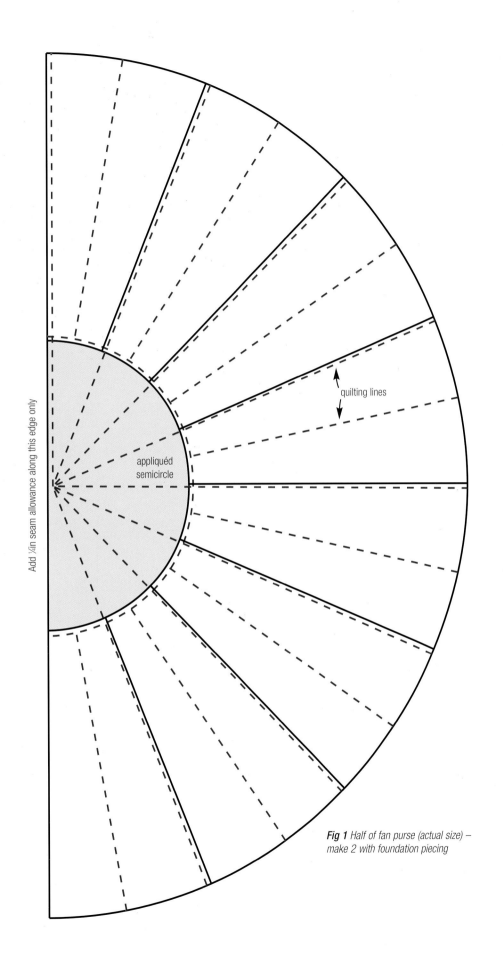

Add ¼in seam allowance along this edge only

appliquéd
semicircle

quilting lines

Fig 1 Half of fan purse (actual size) –
make 2 with foundation piecing

Constructing the Bag

3 **Sewing the binding:** Using the bias cut strip, make double bias binding (see bindings page 106). Pin and machine sew the binding around the edge of the bag panel, being careful not to stretch the binding. When the machine stitching is complete, fold the bias binding over and slipstitch it in place all around the bag panel.

4 **Inserting the zip:** Fold the bag panel in half, right sides together and temporarily slipstitch the zip opening closed along the bound edge. Leave the first and last 2½in of the bag edge unsewn. It is not possible to tack (baste) the zip opening closed in the usual way because there are no raw edges.

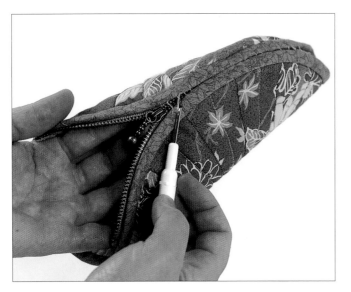

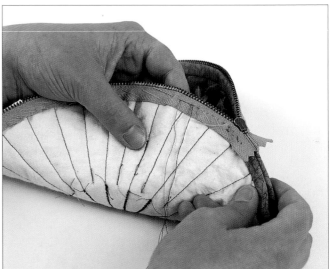

5 Follow the steps on page 108 for inserting a zip invisibly and tack (baste) the zip in place. Turn the bag right side out through one of the open ends. Carefully remove the slipstitching holding the zip opening closed, so the zip can be opened partly while it is permanently sewn in place.

6 Hand sew the zip in place from the wrong side, in running stitch or backstitch, sewing the zip to the back of the bias binding seam. Open the zip to make sewing easier. Once finished, remove the zip tacking (basting).

tip

Line this bag with waterproof nylon if you plan to use it for make-up. Add an interlining if the nylon is slightly transparent.

7 **Making the lining:** Finish constructing the bag by oversewing (whip stitching) the open ends. Then take the circle of lining fabric, turn under a ¼in hem allowance and slipstitch it to the back of the binding seam inside the bag, following the curve at the top of the bag. Turn the bag right side out.

Variation

A larger purse makes a handy travelling vanity bag. The Art Deco design in reproduction fabrics is another variation on the basic Log Cabin foundation piecing method. I drew the design on greaseproof paper (wax paper), pieced the patchwork from the back and removed the paper at the end (see foundation piecing on paper page 100). I surrounded the single central piece with strips in a chic, restricted colour palette for a look reminiscent of 1930s vacation style.

Rice Sack Bag

This bag is one of the first I made, so called because it reminds me of a sack of rice. Its large capacity is great for fabric shopping and I often seem to carry more things than I really need. Matching the Tough Tote, this version has five 6in blocks, Churn Dash and Thrifty, assembled into a strip and machine quilted. The bag's unusual shape is made by folding and stitching the main bag panel without a gusset, with the zip sewn directly into the body of the bag. Make the strap long enough to go across your body and the bag sits neatly at your hip.

You Will Need

Add seam allowances to all fabric and wadding sizes – see page 5

- Patchwork blocks from fabric scraps:
  three 6in square Churn Dash blocks
  two 6in square Thrifty blocks
  two pieces 6in x 2in to co-ordinate

- Checked fabric pieces:
  two 4½in x 34in for bag panel sides
  one 5in x 40in for strap

- Backing fabric 6in x 34in

- 2oz cotton wadding (batting) 6in x 34in

- Lining fabric 15in x 34in

- One 12in zip

- Sewing and quilting threads to tone
  with patchwork

Making the Patchwork

1 Begin by making three Churn Dash blocks and two Thrifty blocks, using **Fig 1** (scaled up to 6in squares). Each nine-patch block is made from an assortment of strips, squares and triangle squares (see Seminole patchwork and triangle squares pages 97-8). Machine sew the five blocks together into one patchwork piece, alternating the blocks. Sew the two 6in x 2in pieces of co-ordinating fabric to the ends. With the wadding (batting) and backing, make a quilt sandwich (see page 103) and then machine quilt (page 103), following the dashed lines in Fig 1.

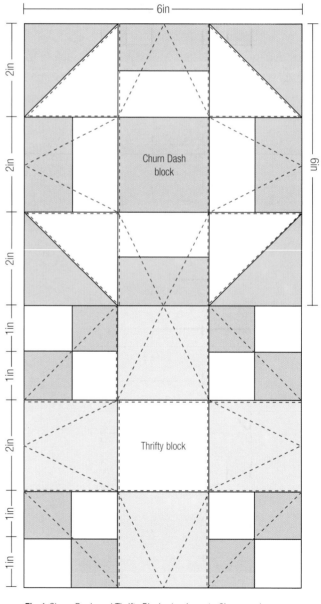

Fig 1 Churn Dash and Thrifty Blocks (scale up to 6in square) – make 3 Churn Dash and 2 Thrifty

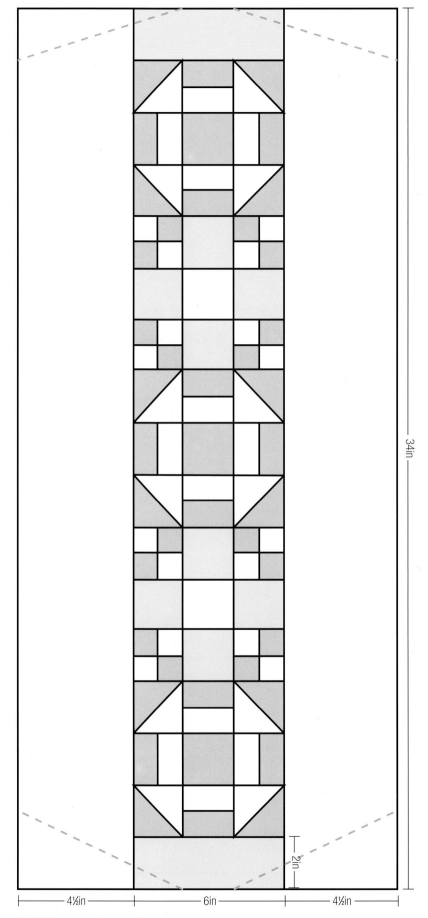

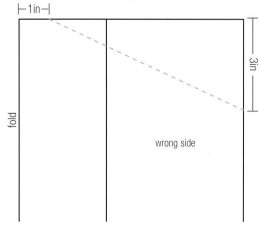

idea

Add a pocket to the patchwork strip, positioning the bottom edge less than 14in from the end of the lower panel (any lower and the pocket will be underneath the bag). A narrow pocket, with a zip or flap fastening, would be ideal for a mobile phone.

Fig 2 *Main bag panel – make 1*

Fig 3 *Sewing diagonal lines on each end of the folded bag panel*

Constructing the Bag

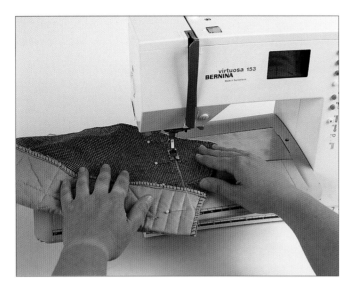

2 Using the checked fabric pieces and following **Fig 2**, machine sew one piece to each side of the patchwork to make the bag panel and topstitch (see Tip). Fold the bag panel in half lengthwise and mark diagonal lines on each end, as shown in **Fig 3**. Machine sew along the diagonal lines, starting ½in from the edge on the side of the bag panel with a few backstitches and sewing right up to the edge at the point. These lines give the top of the bag its unusual pointed shape.

tip Make the bag extra strong by top stitching ⅛in away from the seam line on the bag panel. The seam allowances should be pressed towards the sides.

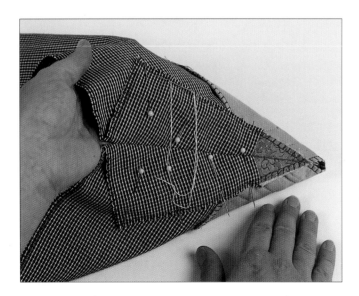

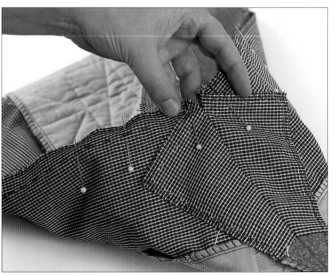

3 Press the diagonal seams open. The seam allowances fold back to form two triangles that keep the top of the bag in shape. Pin and slipstitch these triangles in place. The very top of each point is left open at this stage.

4 **Inserting the zip:** Fold the panel in half, right sides together, and line up the opening where the zip will be sewn. Line up the two diagonal seams at the ½in left unsewn. Pin and tack (baste) the zip opening closed with a ½in seam allowance for 6in on either side of the diagonal seams to allow the seam to be pressed open when you insert the zip. Continue pinning along one side. Machine sew with a ½in seam allowance to create one side seam. The other side seam is sewn after the zip is inserted.

5 Tack (baste) the zip to the back of the tacked seam, with the closed end of the zip at the end of the stitched side seam (see inserting a zip invisibly page 108). Remove the tacking (basting) holding the zip opening closed and machine sew the zip in place. The unsewn side seam gives easier access to sewing the zip and you can unfasten the zip as you sew.

6 Pin and sew the remaining side seam, with a ⅛in seam allowance. Assemble the lining the same way as the bag, leaving the zip opening unsewn.

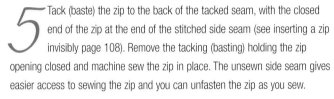

tip

The ends of the zip opening can be reinforced with a bar tack (see Stitch Library page 112).

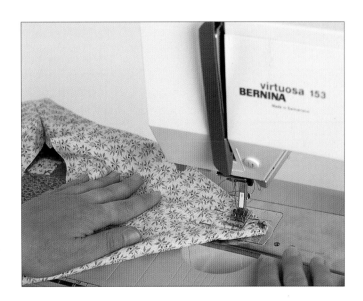

7 **Inserting the lining:** Turn the bag right side out and place it inside the lining. Push the top points of the bag up into the top points of the lining. Use the opening at the point to check that the bag and lining seams are lined up. Pin and machine sew across the point ¼in from the end of the seam, sewing bag and lining together. This will be hidden inside the top of the bag after the strap is attached.

8   Turn the bag and lining right side out. Push the bottom corners of the lining into the bottom corners of the bag. Check that the bag side seam and lining side seam align on both sides. Fold the first bottom corner point to form a right angle, with the side seam running into the point in the centre. Mark a line at right angles to the side seam, 2½in from the point, then pin and machine sew across, sewing the bottom corner of the bag and lining together and creating a triangular flap of fabric. Fold this flap up against the side seam and hand slipstitch to the bag side along the edge. For extra reinforcement, big stitch through all layers ¼in from the flap edge.

9   **Making the strap:** With the 5in x 40in piece of fabric make a tube strap (see page 109), leaving both ends open. Pin this to the top of the bag at the point, with the raw end 1in from the top of the point. Machine sew across the strap, fold the strap upwards and stab stitch through all layers to hold the strap firmly in place. Slipstitch the strap edges to the top point of the bag on either side of the stab-stitched area. Repeat for the other end of the strap, making sure the strap is not twisted.

idea

Sew on the strap and experiment with various patterns stab stitched through all the layers. Decorative patterns based on herringbone and radiating stitches can look effective (see Stitch Library page 112).

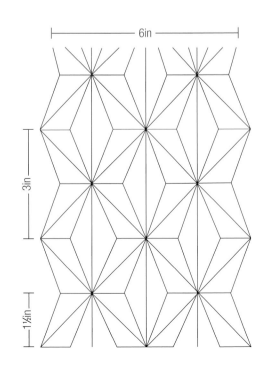

Variation

Ikat fabric and African wax prints go together well, large-scale prints like these giving an interesting, fragmented effect to the patchwork. For this variation the fabrics were cut into strips of random widths and I used the stitch and flip method (see page 99) to sew them straight on to the backing fabric without any wadding (batting). The quilting pattern shown left is an elongated version of the Japanese sashiko hemp leaf design, worked in thick red thread.

Inside
Outside Bag

Small drawstring bags like this are popular kimono
accessories in Japan and I was given a number of
them when I lived there. The square base effect is a
traditional design but I realized it could be developed
into a fully reversible bag. Only three fabrics were
used – two large prints and a plain red – and the
triangle square method was used to make basic
blocks. I added appliqué circles to four of these and
then machine quilted the panels with metallic thread.
You can use the bag with the circle blocks on the
outside or turn it inside out for blocks without circles
– two bags in one!

You Will Need

Add seam allowances to all fabric and wadding sizes – see page 5

- Ten 4in patchwork blocks from print and plain fabrics:
  six double triangle squares
  four double triangle squares with appliqué circles
- Two patchwork strips 20in x 4in from print fabrics
- Muslin pieces for backing four 20in x 4in
- 2oz cotton wadding (batting) four 20in x 4in

- 30in fine viscose chainette cord for loops
- Two 30in lengths of thin cord for drawstrings
- Sewing and quilting threads to tone with patchwork
- Metallic machine embroidery threads
- Metallic machine needle

Making the Patchwork

1 Begin by making ten double triangle squares (also known as Bow blocks). To work out the size for cutting out the squares, add the seam allowances and then add twice the extra allowance for basic triangle squares to make 5½in (see triangle squares page 98). Cut out five squares in this size in each fabric. With one square of each fabric, make ten triangle squares. Now position two triangle squares right sides together with the two different fabrics facing each other and repeat the steps for making the triangle squares. When the squares are opened out, there will be four triangles in each square, with opposite triangles in the same fabrics, as shown in **Fig 1**. Each finished square will measure 4½in.

   Take four of the double triangle squares and appliqué a 3in diameter circle of the third fabric to each (see tip, right, and also hand appliqué page 102). Make two strips of patchwork with five blocks in each.

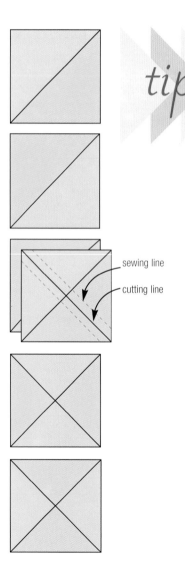

sewing line

cutting line

Fig 1 Making double triangle squares – make 10

tip

Make easy appliqué circles by using a cardboard template ½in smaller than the fabric circles. Run a gathering thread around each fabric circle, gather up the edge around the template to make a neat turning allowance and press. Remove the template, pin the appliqué fabric to the background block and hand stitch in place.

2 Make two strips of patchwork 20in x 4in from 2in x 4in pieces of the two prints (see **Fig 2**). Using the wadding (batting) and backing fabric, sandwich each strip (see making a quilt sandwich page 103). Mark quilting lines on each patchwork panel following the dashed lines in Fig 2 and machine quilt in gold metallic thread. The double triangle squares and the 2in x 4in pairs are quilted in the same four-leaf design. Contrast straight stitch quilting with a fancy stitch for the edge of the circles.

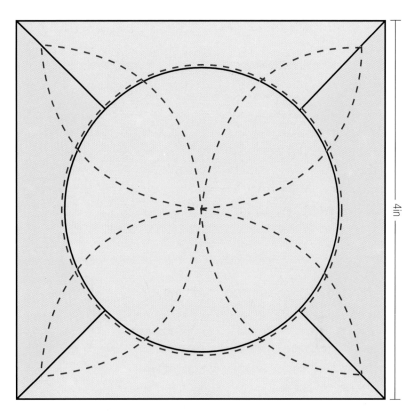

Fig 2 Double triangle square with appliquéd circle and quilting pattern (actual size)

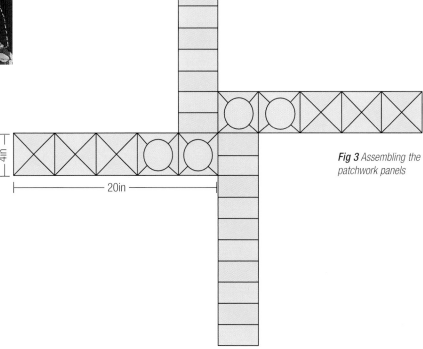

Fig 3 Assembling the patchwork panels

Constructing the Bag

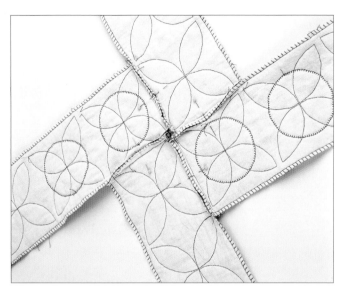

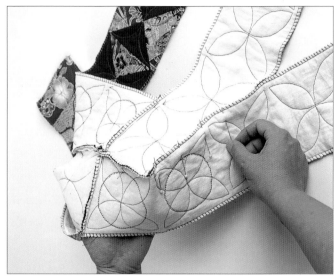

3 Assemble the four patchwork panels as shown in **Fig 3**. Machine sew two strips together at right angles, starting and finishing all seams ¼in from the edge (to enable seams at the centre of the base to lie flat). Start and finish each seam with a few backstitches for added strength. Sew the four strips together to form the base. Press the seams as in the photo – the short edge towards the long edge of the next patchwork piece. Hold in place with herringbone stitch (see page 113) if necessary.

4 Temporarily pin the long side seams. Clip the long edges ⅛in and ease each patchwork around the corner of the neighbouring panel. Check the bag from the right side to make sure the panels are lining up – the horizontal block seams will line up every 4in. When the long seams are pinned in place, the arrangement of the inner bag base will become obvious. Machine sew the inner bag base, repeating step 4. Remove some of the temporary pins to do this.

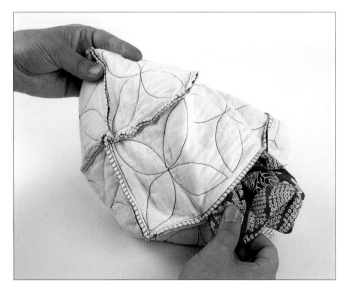

5 Pin the long side seams and machine sew, starting and finishing with a few backstitches. Leave a gap approximately 4in unsewn in the last side seam. Turn the bag right side out through the gap, making sure the base corners are well turned out.

idea

Make the bag as a charm patchwork, with every piece a different fabric from your scrap bag.

6 Push the inside down into the outside of the bag. The fold is the top edge of the bag. Keep this in place by tacking (basting) around three-quarters of the top edge, leaving a gap above the unsewn part of the side seam. Thread a large sharp needle with the fine viscose chainette and tie a knot in the end, large enough not to pull through the patchwork panels. To start and finish, take the needle through the unsewn gap – this will hide the knot within the bag. Make sixteen loops, four per patchwork panel, as shown in **Fig 4**. When the loops are stitched, slipstitch the gap closed. Thread drawstring cord through the loops and tie the ends.

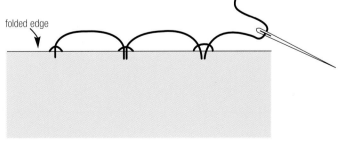

folded edge

Fig 4 Forming chainette loops

Batik Satchel

The satchel is a classic bag and here it takes on a new identity made in wax batik prints, felted wool and leather. I had a basket of these gorgeous fabric scraps that I wanted to use in a special project, emphasizing their vibrant colours and bold patterns. The batiks make the simple Pinwheel blocks really zing and inspired the bright pink lining and strap webbing. The flap conceals a neat patch pocket made from a single Pinwheel. A sashiko-style quilting pattern suggesting leaves decorates the flap and pocket in bright red thread. Keeping the focus on the patchwork and quilting, the satchel fastens with a concealed press-stud under the flap. There is a protective strip of leather on the bottom of the bag and leather detailing – this can be replaced with canvas or synthetic leather if you prefer.

You Will Need

Add seam allowances to all fabric and wadding sizes – see page 5

- Five 4in Pinwheel patchwork blocks from fabric scraps

- Felted wool fabric pieces:
  two 8in x 8in for bag front and back panel
  one 23in x 3in for bag gusset
  one 50in x 3in for strap

- Soft leather pieces (seam allowances already included):
  one 9in x 3½in for bag gusset centre

two 2½in x 3½in for strap ends

- Calico backing fabric pieces:
  three 8in x 8in for flap, front and back
  one 23in x 3in for bag gusset
  one 4in x 4in for patch pocket

- 2oz cotton wadding (batting):
  one 8in x 8in for flap
  one 4in x 4in for patch pocket

- Lining fabric pieces:
  three 8in x 8in for flap, front and back
  one 23in x 3in for bag gusset

- one 4in x 4in for patch pocket

- 50in length of 1½in wide cotton webbing for strap

- 52in length of double bias binding

- Large press-stud fastener

- Sewing and quilting threads to tone with patchwork

- Machine needle for leather

Making the Patchwork

1 Begin by making five 4in Pinwheel blocks. Each block is made from four triangle squares (see page 98). Sew one flap panel with four blocks as in **Fig 1** and reserve one block for the patch pocket, as in **Fig 2**. For each patchwork piece, use one piece of wadding (batting) and one piece of backing to make a quilt sandwich (see page 103). Trim the four corners of the patchwork panel and the bottom corners of the patch pocket to make curves with a 1in radius as in Figs 1 and 2. Hand quilt in big stitch (see page 105), following the dashed lines in the diagrams.

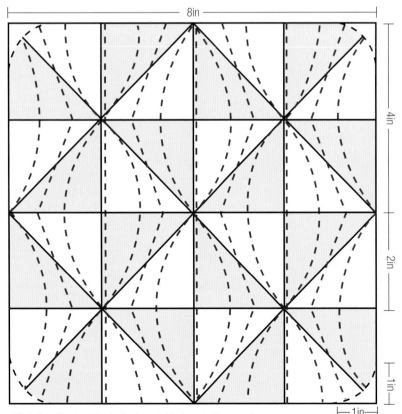

Fig 1 Four Pinwheel blocks (scale each block up to 4in square)

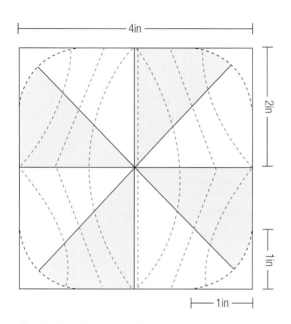

Fig 2 Patch pocket of one pinwheel block

Seams in thicker fabrics like felted wool don't press easily so use steam or a damp pressing cloth. The seam allowance can be held in place flat inside the bag with herringbone stitch (see Stitch Library).

When using large-print fabrics in patchwork, block patterns can seem to 'disappear' when the colours are close in tone. Choose fabrics with high contrasts to keep the patchwork visible or shade colours closely for a colourwash effect.

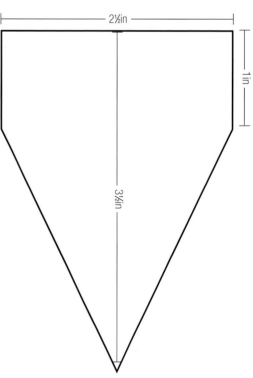

Fig 3 Leather appliqué shape for ends of strap (actual size and extra seam allowances not required) – cut 2

Constructing the Bag

2 **Making the pocket:** Pin the lining fabric to the pocket panel, right sides together, and machine sew across the top of the pocket. Fold the lining over and pin to the back of the pocket panel. Trim the corners of the lining to match the pocket panel curves. Machine sew the lining to the pocket panel around the three remaining edges and bind these edges with bias binding (see making bindings page 106).

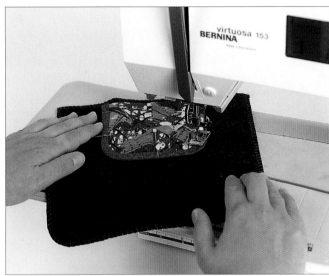

3 Pin the front bag panel on to a piece of calico backing. Trim the bottom corners of the front bag panel to make curves with a 1in radius. Machine sew around the edges. Position the patch pocket on the front bag panel, centred ½in from the top edge. Machine sew the pocket to the panel, stitching just behind the bias-bound edge. Neaten the pocket by slipstitching the edge of the bias binding to the bag panel.

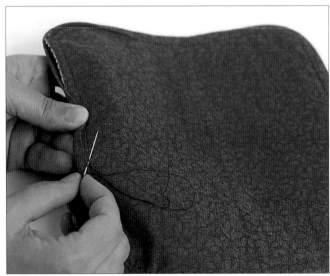

4 **Making the flap:** Pin the lining fabric to the flap, wrong sides together. Following the instructions in step 2, sew the lining fabric to the flap, curving all the corners to the same radius as the pocket and front panel and adding bias binding all round the flap.

5 **Attaching the flap:** Make the back bag panel the same way as the front panel in step 3. Position the flap over the top edge of the back bag panel, overlapping the edge by ¾in and centring on the back panel. Machine sew the flap to the back panel, stitching just behind the bias bound edge, starting and finishing with a few backstitches and without sewing into the corner curves.

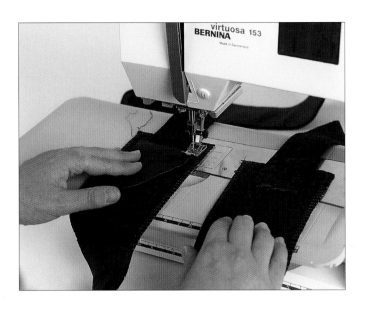
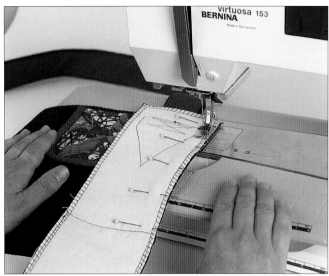

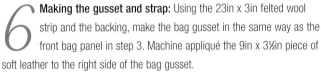

6 **Making the gusset and strap:** Using the 23in x 3in felted wool strip and the backing, make the bag gusset in the same way as the front bag panel in step 3. Machine appliqué the 9in x 3½in piece of soft leather to the right side of the bag gusset.

Using the 50in x 3in felted wool strip and the 50in piece of cotton webbing, make a folded strap (see page 109). Machine sew the strap to the gusset in a figure of eight, lining up the ends of the strap 2in from the top edge of the gusset. Use **Fig 3** as a pattern for two soft leather pieces and machine appliqué over each end of the strap.

7 Pin the gusset to the front panel, right sides together and machine sew down one side. Repeat for the other side. Ease the centre section of the gusset around the curves and the bottom of the front panel and machine sew. Machine sew the back panel to the gusset in the same way as the front panel. Clip the curved corners ⅛in from edge.

tip

Hold leather in place temporarily with adhesive tape and use a leather needle to machine sew the leather appliqué. A leather needle has a sharpened point that pierces the leather. Use it again when stitching the bag seam at this point.

8 **Making the lining:** Make the bag lining the same way as the bag. Machine sew the back main lining panel and then the front lining panel to the gusset lining. When sewing the front lining panel in place, leave a gap approximately 4in unsewn, for bagging out. To sew the lining into the bag, turn the bag right side out. With the lining turned wrong side out, place the bag inside the lining. Machine sew the lining to the bag along the long top edge of the bag sides only. Bag out and slipstitch the unsewn gap closed.

Hand sew one half of the press-stud fastener to the centre bottom edge of the patch pocket just behind the binding. Sew the other half to the bottom centre of the flap lining, taking care not to stitch right through to the front.

Zipover Rucksack

I often used to carry a rucksack when I worked as a footpath officer but this one is strictly for leisure. The zipover design allows easy stowing of a spare sweater or packed lunch. The flapped outer pocket with hook-and-loop strip closure is the right size for most walking maps or a sketchbook and pencils. It's useful for shopping too, especially at big quilt shows when you want both hands free for cameras and catalogues. The foundation-pieced mountain scene, which matches the Quilter's Briefcase, is really just an irregular Log Cabin design. It is machine quilted in simple straight lines to enhance the pictorial effect. The rest of the bag is made from hard-wearing needlecord or corduroy and the back is stiffened with pelmet interfacing. Enjoy the great outdoors!

You Will Need

Add seam allowances to all fabric and wadding sizes – see page 5

- One foundation-pieced patchwork panel 11in x 10in:
  assorted fabric fat eighths and strips
  one piece of foundation stabilizer 12in x 10in

- One patchwork pocket panel 11in x 5½in, from eleven 1in x 5½in strips

- Assorted fabric pieces:
  two 11in x 1½in for pocket flap
  one 11in x 6in for pocket back panel

- Needlecord pieces and lining fabric pieces:
  16in x 11in for back panel (cut 2 for lining)

17¼in x 4in for bag base
32¼in x 1¼in and 32¼in x 3¾in for zip gusset

- Needlecord pieces two 21in x 4⅛in for bag straps

- Pocket lining fabric 11in x 5⅝in

- 11in length of straight grain binding

- Calico backing fabric (for quilted pieces) and 2oz cotton wadding (batting):
  11in x 10in for foundation-pieced patchwork panel
  11in x 5½in for patchwork pocket panel
  11in x 6in for pocket back panel

- Calico backing fabric pieces:
  16in x 11in for bag back panel

17¼in x 4in for bag base
11in x 1½in for pocket flap

- Pelmet interfacing 9in x 15in for bag back panel

- Sewing and quilting threads to tone with patchwork

- 31in zip, double or single pull

- 2in hook-and-loop fastener strip (Velcro)

- Strong cotton or nylon webbing 1¼in wide:
  two 24in lengths (upper straps)
  two 16½in lengths (lower straps)

- Two plastic rucksack buckles to fit webbing width

Making the Patchwork

1 Begin by making the foundation-pieced panel (see foundation piecing page 99). Use **Fig 1** and the picture to help you draw your foundation pattern on greaseproof paper (wax paper), using straight lines to make the landscape. Remove the paper when the patchwork is complete (see Tip below). With wadding (batting) 11in x 10in and backing the same size, make a quilt sandwich (see page 103) and quilt the foundation-pieced panel – continuous machine quilting in the ditch and in zigzags enhances the patchwork, starting and finishing at the edges (see machine quilting page 103).

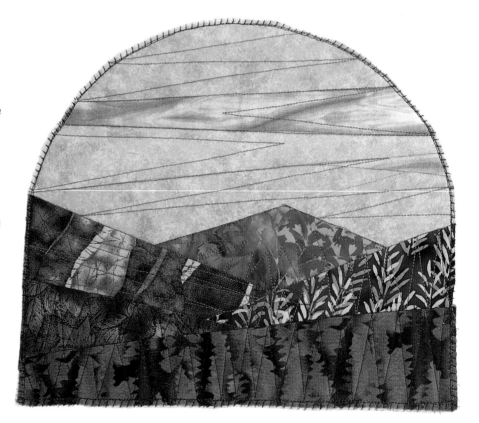

Stitch around the completed foundation piecing ⅛in from the edge to stabilize the bias edges before removing the stabilizer material (if using paper or a tear-off stabilizer) just before layering and quilting.

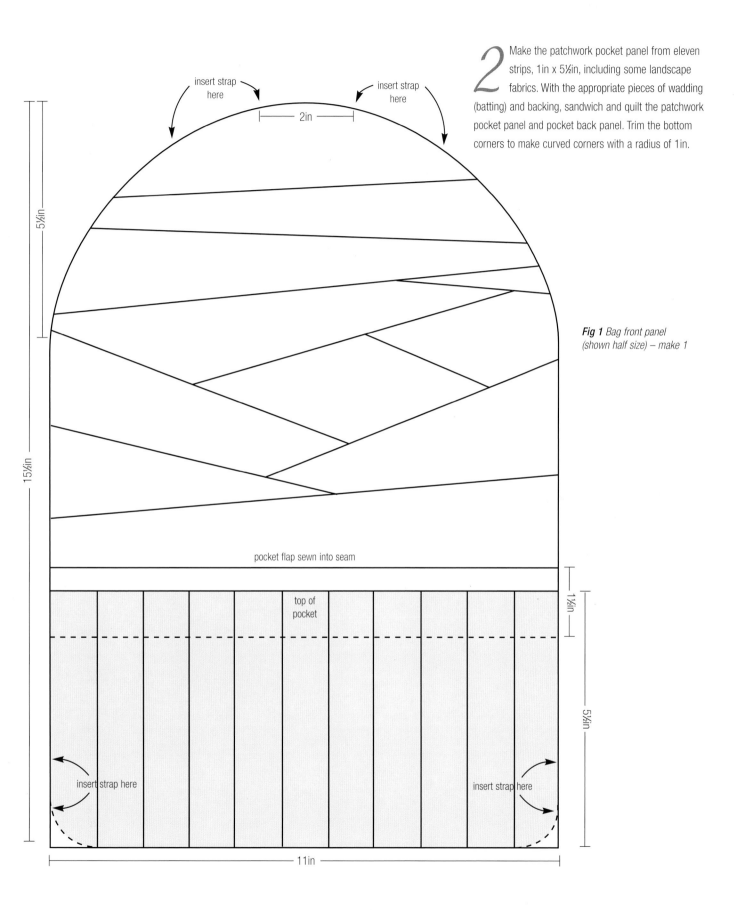

insert strap here

insert strap here

2in

5½in

15½in

2 Make the patchwork pocket panel from eleven strips, 1in x 5½in, including some landscape fabrics. With the appropriate pieces of wadding (batting) and backing, sandwich and quilt the patchwork pocket panel and pocket back panel. Trim the bottom corners to make curved corners with a radius of 1in.

Fig 1 Bag front panel
(shown half size) – make 1

pocket flap sewn into seam

top of pocket

1½in

5½in

insert strap here

insert strap here

11in

Constructing the Bag

3 Making the pocket: Place the wrong side of the pocket lining to the wrong side of the patchwork pocket panel and machine sew around the edges. Pin the straight binding to the pocket top, machine sew, fold over and finish by hand sewing (see making bindings page 106).

Make the pocket flap by placing two flap pieces right sides together, place calico backing on the wrong side of the outer flap fabric and machine sew together along one long side. Open the flap out flat and place the hook side of the hook-and-loop tape on the right side of the strip that will be the underneath of the flap when assembled (this is the side shown in the photograph). The stitching will be hidden from the flap front. Line the tape right up to the seam and machine sew in place. Fold the flap wrong sides together and machine sew around the remaining edges. Sew the loop side of the hook-and-loop tape to the centre of the patchwork pocket panel, just below the binding, so it will line up with the flap.

idea Make smaller pockets by dividing the pocket panel vertically. Simply machine sew vertical rows after placing the patchwork pocket panel on the pocket back panel.

4 Place the patchwork pocket panel on the pocket back panel, right sides up, and pin to make the pocket. Place the pocket flap on the pocket, lining up the top edge with the pocket back panel and tack (baste) to complete making the pocket. Machine sew the completed pocket to the lower edge of the foundation-pieced patchwork panel to make the bag front panel as shown in Fig 1.

5 Making the zip gusset: Place the two zip gusset pieces right sides together and machine sew only ¾in of the seam at each end of one long side. Tack (baste) the remainder of the seam and press open. Tack the zip in place along the seam between the two zip gusset pieces and machine sew the zip (see inserting a zip invisibly page 108). Now machine sew the bag base panel to the backing and sew to each end of the zip gusset to make a continuous loop.

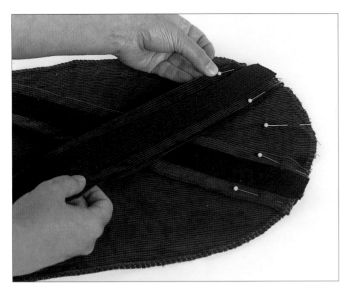

6 **Making the straps:** For each strap, fold up ½in at one end of the strap fabric and fold the long sides to meet in the middle (see folded strap page 109). Thread one half of the rucksack buckle on to the webbing and double the webbing back on itself. Lay the webbing along the folded strap, with 1in of the raw edge at the buckle end tucked in between the main length of webbing and the fabric strap, and pin in place. Machine sew the edge of the webbing to the folded fabric strap, starting at the top end and using a figure of eight stitching pattern to secure the other end of the webbing before sewing back to the top along the opposite edge of the webbing (see attaching straps and D-rings page 110). Machine sew across the two layers of webbing immediately behind the buckle to keep it in place. Pin each strap in place at the top of the rucksack, as shown in Fig 1 and tack (baste) in place. The straps will be sewn in place when the bag is assembled.

7 Machine zigzag one end of each shorter piece of webbing to prevent fraying. (Nylon webbing may be heat sealed across the ends.) Pin the short straps to the bag sides, as shown in Fig 1, and tack (baste) in place. The other halves of the buckles can be threaded on when the bag is complete. These straps will also be sewn in place when the bag is assembled.

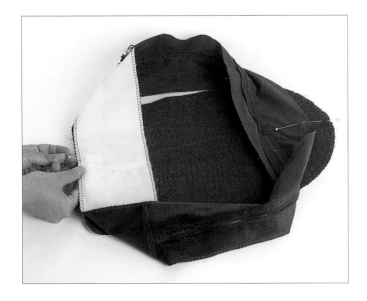

8 **Final bag assembly:** Sew the backing fabric to the wrong side of the bag back panel. Place the strip of pelmet interfacing down the centre of the bag back panel and machine quilt in place, in straight lines at ¾in intervals – use the ribs in the needlecord as stitching guides. Pin the completed gusset to the bag back panel, right sides together. Line up the centre top and bottom of the gusset with the top and bottom of the back panel, pin in place and machine sew. Ease the gusset around the curves at the bottom of the back panel. Sew the completed front panel to the gusset in the same way. (Note: the straps have been omitted in the photograph for clarity.)

9 **Making the lining:** Using the pieces of lining fabric, make the lining in the same way as making the bag. Follow step 5, leaving the zip seam unsewn, and step 8. Place the bag wrong side out inside the lining and slipstitch the lining to the back of zip gusset. Turn to the right side.

Equipment and Materials

Equipment

There are many gadgets and gizmos available for today's quilter but you don't have to buy all of them for the projects in this book! If you are a quilter already you will probably have everything you need. If not, make sure you have the following basics.

1 Rotary Cutter

Rotary cutting has revolutionized the way patchwork is cut out, allowing quicker cutting, precision piecing without cutting templates and machine sewing with the quarter inch foot (using the cut fabric edge as a guide). Cutters come in various sizes – 28mm and 45mm blades are the most popular. Make sure the blade is clean and sharp as dull, nicked blades will skip threads and make cutting difficult. All cutters have a blade set at the end of a handle with a safety guard, operated by a click or squeeze action depending on the cutter. The safety guard is very important as the blade is *extremely* sharp, so make a habit of replacing the guard after *every* cut. Information on rotary cutting is on page 96.

2 Cutting Mat

A self-healing cutting mat is essential for use with your rotary cutter, to protect your table and make sure your cutter blade stays sharp. There are various brands available. Choose a mat marked with imperial measurements and use the measurements on the mat to help you cut larger pieces. Cutting mats are tough but they can be damaged. Store flat, away from heat and direct sunlight and prolong its life by cutting smaller pieces on different areas of the mat's surface. Only use your mat with your rotary cutter – use a different mat for paper crafts as craft knives can nick the surface.

3 Quilter's Ruler

This transparent, wider-than-average ruler marked with a grid is an indispensable tool, both for rotary cutting and for marking quilting patterns in straight lines. Imperial quilt rulers are divided into inches and fractions of an inch, to ⅛in or even ⅟₁₆in. Many have 45 and 60 degree lines too. Rulers 4½in and 6½in wide are the most useful for projects in this book. Select a ruler with clear markings and stick to the same rule throughout a project. There can be slight variations between one ruler and another, even of the same brand, and this may result in your patchwork

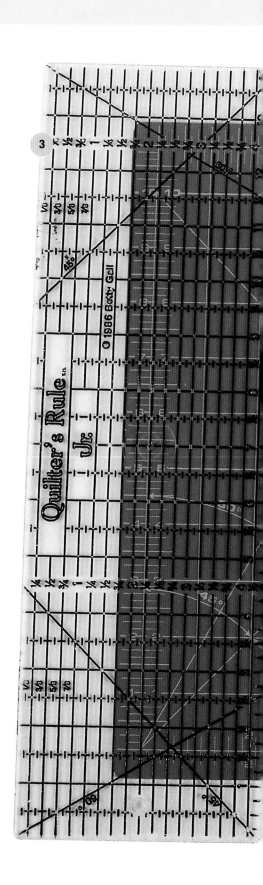

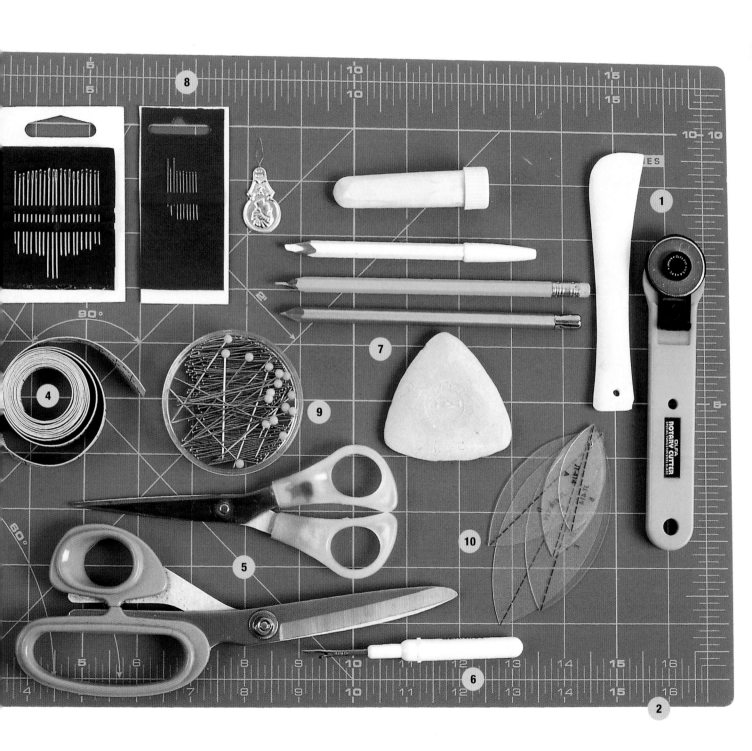

pieces not fitting together accurately. Make sure your ruler can't slip while you are cutting. Some rulers have a raised grid or gripper dots on the wrong side to hold your fabric steady, or add your own self-adhesive grips.

4 Tape Measure

A good quality tape measure is needed for measuring straps and around curves.

5 Scissors

Keep pairs of scissors for particular jobs. You will need a large pair of sewing scissors for cutting out curves, cutting braid and other similar tasks. Reserve your best quality sewing scissors for fabric. A 'second-best' pair should be used for cutting wadding (batting), as some can blunt scissors. A small pair of embroidery scissors or thread snips makes trimming threads easy. Use paper scissors for cutting out templates for appliqué and quilting patterns.

6 Seam Ripper

This gadget is also known as a quick unpick and is often supplied in your sewing machine tool kit. It is excellent for removing tacking (basting) after inserting zips. If you make a mistake and need to use it to unpick a bag assembly seam, take care and remove a stitch at a time.

7 Fabric Markers

Fabric markers should be easy to use, easy to see and easy to remove after you have finished sewing. You will use them to mark some sewing lines in bag assembly and to mark quilting patterns, so you will need a variety of colours to contrast with your fabrics. Tailor's chalk, quilter's marking pencils

and Chaco liners (chalk wheels) are available in several colours. A *hera*, a traditional Japanese fabric marker made of bone, polishes a line on the cloth that remains until the item is washed and can be useful for darker fabrics. A thin sliver of soap also marks well on dark cloth.

8 Sewing Needles and Threader

Hand and machine needles are available for many purposes and in many sizes. Use sharps for general hand sewing and betweens for hand quilting. If you find smaller betweens difficult to hold, use a sharp for your hand quilting too. Crewel needles are used for embroidery and will make big stitch quilting and embellishment with embroidery threads easier. Use an appropriate machine needle for your work and change it frequently – immediately if damaged or bent, or if your machine starts skipping stitches or after several hours of stitching. I use a regular point needle size 80/11 for patchwork and bag assembly. Match your needle to your thread type (see box page 105) – metallic, embroidery and jeans needles all have larger eyes to sew threads that would snap in a regular needle. Needles for leather have sharpened points.

9 Pins

Quilting pins are long and fine, usually with a glass head. Use them when assembling bags and pin at right angles to the seam you are sewing. They can also be used for pin basting the quilt sandwich.

10 Templates

Ready-made templates in simple shapes can be used to mark quilting patterns, such as leaves, hearts and

circles, or you can cut your own from cardboard or clear template plastic. Circles in various sizes are used to round off bag corners.

Iron

You will need an iron and an ironing surface for pressing patchwork and bag assembly. Press patchwork with a dry iron to avoid distortion (see page 97). A travel iron is handy for pressing patchwork blocks. Use a steam iron to press bag assembly seams after each stage of construction.

Sewing Machine

You will need a reliable lockstitch sewing machine that can sew straight stitches and zigzag. Utility stitches and a small range of embroidery stitches are also useful. Free motion machine quilting is not used in any of the bag projects so there is no need to be able to drop or cover the feed dogs. There are a number of domestic machines

made for quilters that are supplied with specialized presser feet (see picture below) and a range of stitches useful for quilting but most modern machines will be adequate. Use the correct foot for the stitch and test tension on a scrap of fabric before you begin. A walking foot (not illustrated) is necessary for smooth straight-line machine quilting on larger quilts. It helps to eliminate puckers by feeding all the layers in the quilt sandwich through at the same rate. I don't use one for bag making, as the patchwork and quilted panels are small and the layers do not tend to shift – but if you like it, use it! Some machines have a 'free arm' feature, where the flat machine bed can be removed. This is really designed for dressmaking procedures but can make sewing curved sections of bags easier. If you are not familiar with your machine, work through the instruction manual or consult the machine dealer.

Presser feet (left to right):
Standard straight stitch/zigzag foot – for general sewing, utility and embroidery stitches. Use for machine quilting as the wide foot covers the feed dogs adequately.
Zipper foot – for sewing in zips and piping.
Quilting guide bar – for quilting parallel lines and grids. The guide bar slots into the back of the machine foot.
Quarter inch foot – essential for accurate patchwork. Can be bought separately and may vary slightly between different manufacturers.

Materials

If you already enjoy quilting or dressmaking, you probably have a lot of fabric pieces and offcuts in your scrap box that would be ideal for making bags. Quilters may even have spare patchwork blocks left over from another project. Slightly heavier curtain materials and lightweight furnishing fabrics can also be used for certain parts of bags.

▶ Fabrics

Cotton This fabric is the easiest to use for patchwork, with or without prints. Many fabrics are produced especially for patchwork and are often sold ready-cut in 'fat quarters' (a yard of fabric quartered) or 'fat eighths'. These are easy to cut and sew, don't fray too readily and can be pressed to a sharp crease. Use new fabrics for a long-lived bag. Polycotton blends and pure synthetics are not suitable for traditional patchwork – I find they either don't crease when pressed or become creased too easily.

Silk This is trickier to use than cotton because it frays easily and may be slippery or stretchy, depending on the weave. Choosing the right technique can help. I used foundation piecing for the silk and cotton Envelope Bag.

Other fabrics Fabrics used for the non-patchwork sections of the bags (such as the zip strips and around the patchwork sections) can be heavier – tough denim, canvas, needlecord and lightweight furnishing can all be used. Again, think about the use of the bag. If you want to be able to wash your bag, use washable fabrics. Check that fabrics can be ironed to a sharp crease, as assembling your bag can be difficult with crease-resistant fabric. Dressmaking and home furnishing shops can be a good source of interesting fabrics – often the bargain basket has a useful assortment of pieces.

Backing fabrics In the quilt sandwich these are behind the wadding. The backing shows on the reverse of a patchwork quilt but is hidden in bags by the linings. A crisp backing fabric, like firm calico, would make a bag more rigid and would be harder to hand quilt. Use it for bags such as the Tough Tote or Quilter's Travel Bag. Lightweight cottons and muslin give a softer effect and are easy to hand quilt even in big stitch, as seen in the Inside Outside Bag and the Rice Sack Bag.

Lining fabrics Linings protect the back of the patchwork and quilting from the bag's contents. They are best made from plainer fabrics and less 'busy' prints, as heavy patterns can camouflage the contents, especially in handbags. Solid colours can look good, co-ordinating with the main bag fabrics. Waterproof linings (like ripstop nylon) may be useful for some bags, beach bags for example.

▶ Threads

Sewing threads You will need good quality cotton thread for sewing patchwork and for bag assembly, with softer

When choosing fabrics think about the use your bag will have – a tough shopping bag in delicate fabrics would not last long! Bearing such frequent use in mind, it could be a waste to make your everyday bag from recycled, vintage fabric: save your precious, old fabrics for an evening or special-occasion bag.

Polyester wadding

This is generally easier to hand quilt through than cotton wadding but some, such as compressed 6oz polyester waddings, will need to be machine quilted. Polyester waddings are often too slippery for machine quilting. It can be high or low loft, giving a puffy or flat appearance to your quilting.

Cotton wadding
This is good for machine quilting because it doesn't slip around in the quilt 'sandwich' of patchwork, wadding and backing. Almost all cotton waddings shrink when washed (by up to 5%), so pre-soak the wadding and tumble dry on a low heat setting if you don't want a puckered surface for that antique look. Cotton wadding gives a flatter, low loft appearance. It can be hand quilted too.

Wool wadding
This is a traditional hand quilting wadding and also the most expensive. I keep my wool offcuts for larger quilts as, with care, small pieces can be combined.

If you love hand quilting wool wadding, use it for a soft bag. It is likely to shrink when washed.

Blended wadding
Blended 80/20 waddings are now available, with 80% cotton and 20% polyester. There are also machine waddings with a layer of cotton scrim or muslin which prevents stretch.

▶ Notions and Fasteners
You will need various notions and fasteners, including zips, buttons, webbing, D-rings, cords and poppers – see individual bag instructions for exact requirements.

Buttons
These make attractive fasteners and are available in various materials. Choose large buttons and buttons with shanks and toggles that fasten and unfasten easily. Loop-and-ball fasteners are available ready-made (see Long Workbag) or you can make your own from toggles and braid.

Zips
These are mostly the closed-end type but open-end zips sold for jackets can be used by stitching in the ends. Zips with two pulls, like suitcase zips, allow the bag to be opened in the middle of the zip (see Quilter's Briefcase). Choose strong, good

---

tacking (basting) threads for temporary stitching. Brown, dark blue, grey, beige and other neutral tones are the most useful for patchwork, co-ordinating with most colour mixtures. I do not recommend polyester as a general sewing thread because it is stronger than the cotton fibres and can eventually cut through fabric. Machine quilting shows up least with invisible nylon thread or can be emphasized with rayon or metallic threads (see Inside Outside Bag). Try multicoloured cotton threads too. Jeans thread is effective for hand quilting and topstitching, especially with denim fabrics (see Quilter's Workbag).

Embroidery threads Thicker threads including cotton perlé, Japanese sashiko thread and cotton à broder are good for hand-quilted big stitch and embroidered embellishment. You can also use multicoloured threads to accent your work (see Double Bottle Bag variation page 23). Wind skeined embroidery threads on to cards or empty thread spools before use.

▶ Wadding
If you make larger quilted projects, save offcuts of wadding (batting) as there is often enough for a bag. I store small offcuts in the original packaging for easy identification. Otherwise, quilt wadding is sold in standard sizes and by the yard. A variety of waddings are available in polyester, cotton, wool and blends and for hand or machine quilting. Wadding is rated by weight. Unlike choosing wadding for bed quilts, warmth is not an issue when bag making. Most of the bags were wadded with 2oz or equivalent, although thicker wadding can be used to protect a bag's contents. Match the wadding to the quilting technique – read the label or ask your supplier.

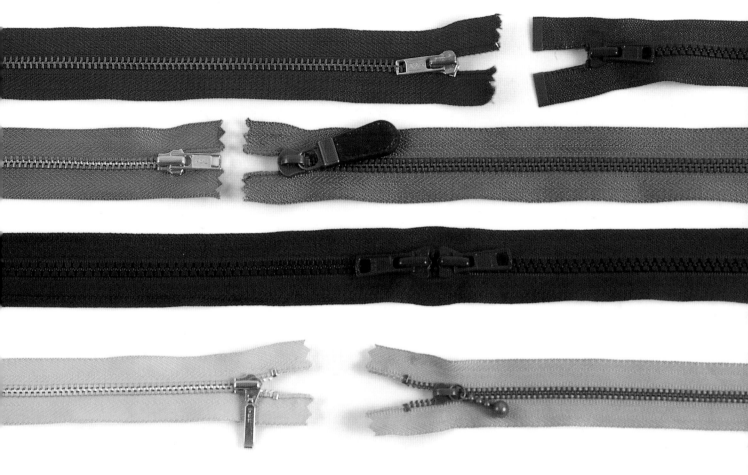

quality zips as bag zips are opened and closed more often than zips on clothing and need to be tough. Some zips have fancy pulls or you can add tassels or beads.

Webbing This makes good straps and handles and is available in a range of colours and widths in tough nylon. Plastic buckles, used on rucksacks (sometimes called parachute clips), are made to fit standard webbing widths. Thinner cotton webbing can be sewn on to fabric to make a stronger strap (see Batik Satchel) or you could experiment with fancy braids. Ready-made straps and handles are sometimes available in craft shops and some bags can be adapted to

use these. Try recycling a strong belt, keeping the buckle to adjust the length.

Cords and piping Cords make straps for dainty bags and can be threaded through eyelets (see Envelope Bag variation page 11). The cord should not be too stretchy. All but the smallest eyelets are made with two parts and are supplied in packs with eyelet tools and instructions. If you don't want to insert eyelets yourself, shoe and bag repair shops will do it for you. You can make a co-ordinated cord yourself

by twisting, plaiting or braiding. Cord is also used to provide body for fabric piping, inserted into seams. Piping is functional as well as decorative, reinforcing seams and protecting the edges of the bag from excessive wear.

D-rings and clips These are available in different sizes. Check that they fit your strap or webbing at the time of purchase. The clips are known by various names, including hipster clips and swivels.

Popper fasteners These fasteners are easy for young children to use. They are made in four parts and, like eyelets, are inserted with the special tool supplied. They may be sold as anorak poppers. Hook-and-loop tape (sold under the trade name 'Velcro' in the UK) is also easy to use. Large press-studs are another unobtrusive fastener.

▶ Embellishments

Embellishments can jazz up your bags wonderfully. Use beads, buttons, sequins and other embellishments, which should be applied after the patchwork and quilting is complete but before the flat bag panels are assembled. Choose embellishments that accent and harmonize with your fabrics and the intended use of your bag (see Tough Tote variation page 17).

Notions are available in various colours and materials, so remember to co-ordinate finishes for a professional look. If you can't find the fabric or notions you want in your local quilting shop, extend your searches – here are some possibilities:

▶ **Outdoor sports shops**
for rucksack and tent spares, ideal for zips and clips, webbing, very strong cords and lines (sold for rock climbing).

▶ **Furnishing fabric shops**
strong fabrics for non-pieced sections of bags, long zips, zips by the yard (sold for loose covers).

▶ **Upholsterers**
for long zips and zips by the yard.

▶ **Dressmaking haberdashers**
for buttons, loop-and-ball fasteners, beads.

▶ **Shoe and bag repair shops**
for hipster and swivel clips, eyelet and popper insertion services.

▶ **Hardware shops**
for strong webbing and cord.

Techniques

If you are an experienced quilter, you will already know how to make patchwork and quilt it, but for beginners this section describes all the basic patchwork, quilting and bag making techniques used in this book. I have avoided unnecessary repetition as much as possible, so some techniques that are used only once are included in the relevant bag project. Stitches used when making the bags are illustrated in the Stitch Library, beginning on page 112.

Patchwork Techniques

Traditional patchwork blocks are used for many of the bags. You may have blocks left over from another quilting project that you can use or you may need to start from scratch if you are a beginner. I mostly used my favourite blocks that are quick and easy to rotary cut and assemble by machine. A standard quarter inch seam allowance all round is added to all patchwork pieces when cutting out and you can sew this allowance accurately with the quarter inch foot on your sewing machine for accurate patchwork without templates. For more ideas on blocks to use, see the Block Library beginning on page 116.

The patchwork techniques covered in this section describe all you need to know to make the patchwork for the bags and include cutting fabric strips, machine piecing techniques, speed piecing triangle squares and flying geese units, foundation piecing methods, hand piecing and appliqué.

▶ Preparing Fabrics

Prepare your fabrics by washing them before use in mild detergent, in case any colours run and to allow for shrinkage. Exceptions to this rule are fabrics which are dry-clean only, such as some silks (in which case remember you will not be able to wash your bag). If the fabrics lack body after washing, iron while damp with a little spray starch. I avoid starches with silicone because it can make fabric slippery.

▶ Cutting Fabric Strips

With the ruler firmly on top of your fabric, square off uneven ends of the fabric before you start and cut off the tightly woven selvage. Cut with the grain of the fabric (with printed stripes and checks, cut with the pattern). Turn your cutting mat through 180 degrees and line up the relevant mark on the ruler – for example, 2½in if 2in is the finished size. Line up your rotary cutter against the ruler's edge and cut. You can cut strips very economically to standard sizes for squares and rectangles, such as 2½in squares and 1½in x 2½in rectangles from the same 2½in strip.

Cutting Safety

The rotary cutter has a *very* sharp blade and it is easy to accidentally cut yourself or others. Please follow these safety tips:

▶ Hold the cutter firmly in the same hand you write with at a 45 degree angle, and hold the ruler in place with your other hand.

▶ Cut with the blade against the side of your ruler – on the right if you are right-handed and on the left if you are left-handed. The patchwork piece you are cutting is under the rule.

▶ Use a sharp blade that is free from nicks and other damage. Using a dull blade requires more pressure when you cut and risks the blade slipping.

▶ Stand up to cut and place the mat on a firm surface – a kitchen counter or sturdy table is ideal.

▶ Always cut away from yourself.

▶ Always replace the safety guard on the cutter – make a habit of doing this after every cut.

▶ Wear something on your feet when you cut, in case you drop the cutter.

▶ Keep cutting equipment away from children and pets.

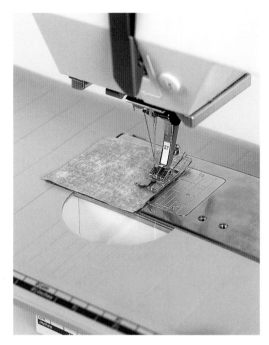

▶ Machine Piecing Patchwork

Place your first two pieces right sides together, making sure the edges to be sewn line up. Set your sewing machine to a slightly shorter than average stitch length and check the tension is even. Use the quarter inch foot and line up the fabric edge with the edge of the foot when you sew. It may help if you sit slightly to the right of the machine needle so you can see this easily. Some quarter inch feet have a guide plate on the right-hand side so the fabric can't be sewn with a wider seam.

Chain piecing is an industrial technique that speeds up piecing patchwork. When you have sewn your first two pieces together, don't cut the thread. Place the next two pieces together and sew them a stitch or two after the first two pieces. Continue like this to make a 'chain' which can be cut up afterwards.

tip

If your machine tends to loop up the first few stitches, use a piece of scrap fabric as a 'leader' when you begin and chain piece the first two patchwork pieces on to that.

▶ Pressing Patchwork

Press each stage of your patchwork as you go along, with the seam allowance to one side as later this will help stop the wadding (batting) from 'bearding' or coming through the seam. Press towards the darker fabric out of preference, as pressing dark towards light can cause a shadow effect on paler fabrics. Pressing in alternate directions makes the seams interlock neatly when the work is assembled and avoids lumpy seams where four layers of the seam allowance meet. Press with a dry iron using an up and down action so the patchwork is not stretched and distorted – you are pressing, not ironing! Good pressing can really make a difference to your patchwork so get it right before you continue piecing.

▶ Seminole Patchwork

This is a machine piecing technique that originated with the American Seminole Indians. It can speed up piecing some patchwork blocks made from squares and rectangles, as in the Rice Sack Bag. Seminole patchwork must be machine sewn because the seams are cut across and hand sewing would come undone.

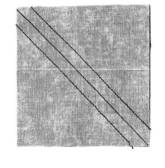

Rotary cut strips to the required width and sew them together. Press the seam to one side. Rotary cut further units across the sewn seam, remembering the seam allowance, then rearrange and sew together. For a 4in four-patch block, you would cut strips and then the units 2½in wide. The finished block would still have a ¼in seam allowance all round, measuring 4½in.

▶ *Triangle Squares*

This speed piecing machine technique allows you to make triangle square elements in a block, as used in the Batik Satchel, without sewing on a cut bias edge, which may distort and spoil your patchwork.

Start by adding an extra ⅞in seam allowance to your two squares (e.g. 2½ + ⅞in = 2⅞in). Draw a diagonal line on the lighter

square and place squares together. Treat this line as the fabric edge, lining it up with the edge of the quarter inch foot, and machine sew. Sew again along the other side of the drawn line and cut along the line. Press towards the darker fabric and clip off the 'dog ears'. This makes two triangle squares. Sew two triangle squares together, repeating the method, to make a four triangle block (see Inside Outside Bag). Blocks that use triangle squares include Churn Dash and Pinwheel.

▶ *Flying Geese*

This is another machine piecing method that avoids sewing on a cut bias edge. The technique was used to create strips of Flying Geese units for the Quilter's Travel Bag.

This easy Flying Geese unit uses a rectangle (the 'goose') on a 2:1 ratio. For a 1in x 2in finished size, add ¼in seam allowance and cut a 1½in x 2½in piece. The triangle (the 'sky') is a made from a square measuring the same size as the shortest side of the rectangle, i.e. 1½in square. Cut two squares for each rectangle. Draw a diagonal line on each square. Place one square on the rectangle and sew along the drawn line. Fold over the triangle you have made and press. Use scissors to trim away the excess fabric underneath and repeat. This makes one unit.

Flying Geese may be sewn together in a strip, as in the Quilter's Travel Bag, and also form part of blocks such as Eight Point Star. There are other methods for making Flying Geese that avoid the tiny amount of waste fabric that is trimmed off but I find this method is good for scrap piecing.

The triangle square and Flying Geese unit methods can be used to build up other blocks, as shown bottom of page – Snowball (left), square on point (top right) and a triangle corner within a triangle square. The Block Library beginning on page 116 includes more ideas.

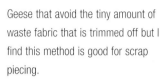

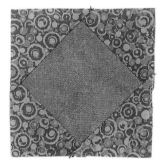
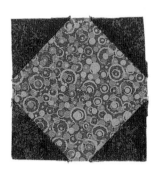
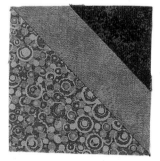

▶ Foundation Piecing

You can make patchwork quickly and accurately with foundation piecing. Pieces are machine sewn together on to a paper or fabric foundation, which stabilizes the fabric. Translucent paper foundations allow piecing from the back so the sewing lines are visible. The stitching perforates the paper so it tears away easily when the piecing is complete. Fabric foundations are left in place as part of the quilt sandwich. Foundation piecing is a good technique for tricky fabrics that fray or stretch easily, especially permanent foundations for silk, as used in the Envelope Bag. The extra stability is also important in more complex designs where the fabric grain may not be consistent, as in the Fan Purse. A range of different specialized stabilizer materials are available but I used calico, cotton flannel or greaseproof paper (wax paper) for the projects in this book – all easy to find. Any crisp, translucent paper that tears off easily could also be used. Press your work with a dry iron at each stage for a crisp finish.

▶ Stitch and Flip Strip

This method is the most basic form of foundation piecing and an easy method for scraps (see Rice Sack Bag variation page 69). Cut a foundation strip the required width and length for your project, remembering to add the seam allowances. Cut an assortment of patchwork pieces in various widths – the length should be the same as the foundation strip width. Place the first piece face up on the end of the foundation strip and line up the edges. Place the second piece face down on the first piece, pin and machine sew the two pieces together with a ¼in seam along the long edge only, through the foundation strip as well. Flip the second piece over so the right side is showing and press. Continue adding pieces in the same way until the whole foundation strip is covered.

▶ Log Cabin

The traditional Log Cabin block develops the stitching and flipping idea further. Exciting random piecing and landscape effects can be achieved by varying the widths and angles of the Log Cabin strips or tapering the pieces (see Zipover Rucksack and Quilter's Briefcase).

1 Mark guidelines for Log Cabin on a fabric or paper backing, for example, consecutive squares at 1in intervals for 1in strips. Cut strips ½in wider than the finished size. The centre square can be the same size as the strip width, in which case the first strip will be the same size as the square, or larger. Pin the centre square piece in place. Log Cabin centres in old quilts are usually a bright or light colour.

2 Pin, machine stitch and flip the first strip. Use the guidelines on the foundation square to help align the strips. The Log Cabin light and dark effect is created by sewing the strips in pairs around the block. Start with light strips if you want the darker tone to predominate and dark strips if you want more light tone in the block. Try contrasting shiny and matt fabrics for a different effect (see Envelope Bag).

3 Pin, machine stitch and flip the second strip. Continue adding strips in this way until the block is complete. Remove any paper.

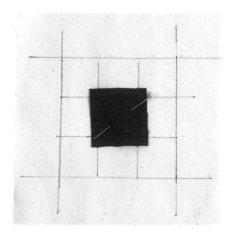

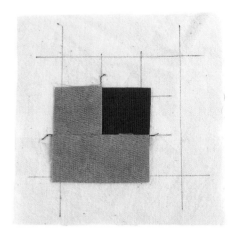

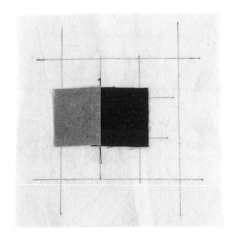

▶ Foundation Piecing on Paper

The fan design is another variation on the simple stitch and flip technique and was used in the Fan Purse.

1 Trace the foundation piecing design on to greaseproof paper (wax paper). Remind yourself which side of the paper is which by writing on the front of the paper only. Number the shapes if you wish. Cut patchwork pieces large enough to cover the shapes generously. The patches do not need to be exact and can be trimmed after stitching. Pin the first fan piece to the front of the foundation paper at

one end of the fan. Turn the paper over and check the fabric covers the first shape with a ¼in or more overlap all round. The pieces are sewn from the back, so pin from the back too and remove the original pin. Anchor the first strip to the end of the fan shape.

2 Position the second piece of fabric. Unlike the basic stitch and flip, the second and subsequent strips are lined up to overlap the stitching line on the foundation paper, not the edge of the first strip. Check the position from the back and pin in place.

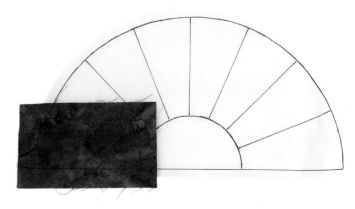

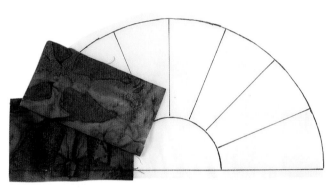

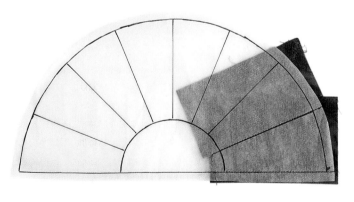

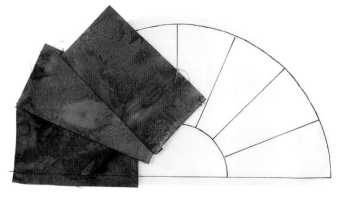

Machine sew along the stitching line on the paper, through the two layers of fabric and paper foundation. Trim the seam allowance to approximately ¼in, flip the piece over and press.

3 Continue piecing the fan. When complete, turn the block over and machine stitch around the edge, about ⅛in away from the drawn edge to stabilize bias edges. This stitching will be hidden in the ¼in seam allowance when the block is finished. Trim around the block, leaving a ¼in seam allowance. To finish making the fan, appliqué (described overleaf) a semicircle of plain fabric to the centre of the fan.

▶ English Paper Piecing

This is a traditional hand sewn method for patchwork using paper templates, as used in the Victorian Circle Bag. Piecing over papers is a good method for making more complex patterns, especially with hexagons and diamonds. The accuracy of the paper determines the finished shape and is more important than the accuracy of the cut fabric. Use graph paper to help you cut perfect shapes. Compatible isometric (triangular) and squared graph paper is made specially for English paper piecing and is available by mail order or from craft shops. Ready-cut shapes are also available.

Pin the shape to your fabric, fold the fabric over the paper edge and tack (baste) it to the paper. Place pieces right sides together and oversew together, starting and finishing with a few stitches in the opposite direction. Remove the papers when the whole patchwork is complete. The seams are left pressed open. Traditional English paper piecing is often left unquilted.

Hexagons are the easiest shape because the corners fold in very neatly. Sew six hexagons around a seventh in a contrasting fabric to make a Grandmother's Flower Garden block.

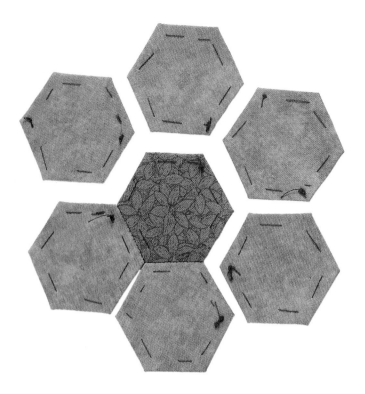

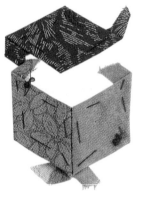

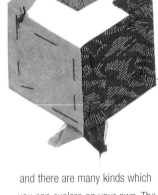

motifs can be cut out and appliquéd for a traditional broderie persé effect.

Hand appliqué

This method can create exciting effects. Raw edge hand appliqué (left in picture below) is popular and produces a soft, feathery edge. It often works best with tightly woven fabrics such as sheeting or lawn. Try using simple shapes with mostly bias edges, sewn on in running stitch or hand embroidery stitches. Cut out the shape without a seam allowance and hand sew to the background.

Needleturn appliqué

This method of appliqué gives a firmer, stronger edge to the appliquéd shape (right in picture below). It uses an appliqué needle or a long sharp to turn under the turning allowance as you sew, using the point of the needle to stroke it into place. Cut out the shape with a ⅛in turning allowance all round and tack (baste) the shape to the background with small stitches ¼in from the cut edge. The tacking stitches prevent too much fabric being turned under. Work with the edge of the appliqué towards you, so you can see your stitches. As most of

the appliqué shape will have a bias edge, it is not necessary to clip the fabric on a curve, just ease it under. Only clip into deep V-shapes and then only a few threads of fabric. Press the turned edge between your fingers as you go along. Start and finish sewing on a long side, sewing the shape to the background with small hemming stitches. An easy method for appliqué circles is given in the tip on page 72.

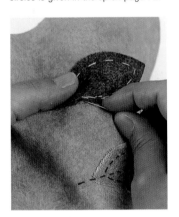

Diamonds are a more difficult shape due to the narrow 60 degree points. Leave the seam allowances on the points. Diamonds in light, medium and dark colours can make a pattern called Tumbling Blocks (see Victorian Circle Bag).

▶ *Appliqué*

Appliqué involves laying and stitching one piece of fabric over another to create a decorative design and the technique is good for enhancing bag designs. Simple appliqué shapes often work best and are sewn to backing fabric by hand or machine. Appliqué is not a patchwork technique but a method in itself

and there are many kinds which you can explore on your own. The techniques described below are those I used for some of the bags.

Fusible web appliqué

Make quick appliqué by ironing a fusible web backing to fabric scraps, cutting out shapes and ironing on to a backing fabric. Decorate raw edges with machine satin or embroidery stitches or simply zigzag with invisible nylon thread. I used this method of appliqué for the Double Bottle Bag variation, page 23. Note: fusible web may stiffen an appliqué motif, making hand sewing difficult. Individual fabric

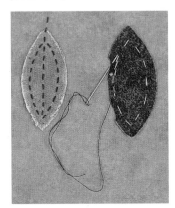

idea

Appliqué with fabric is only one kind of embellishment. Decorate your bag further with embroidery stitches, braids, beads, buttons or whatever takes your fancy!

Quilting Techniques

In this book, some of the bags are completely quilted while others are only quilted in the patchwork sections. This section describes how to mark out a quilting pattern, make a quilt sandwich and quilt the patchwork blocks or the fabric panels of your bags. Quilting may be sewn by hand or machine, each method giving a different effect (see photo overleaf).

▶ Marking a Quilting Pattern

Before you start quilting, you may need to mark the quilting pattern. Use a suitable marker that can be removed later. The bag quilting designs fall into several groups and some do not need marking. You can also invent your own patterns. If you are planning to machine quilt the design, patterns with continuous lines are easier as there is less stopping and starting and fewer ends to finish off.

▶ Quilt along patchwork seam lines, called quilting 'in the ditch', or following the fabric print – neither require marking (see Quilter's Travel Bag).

▶ Quilt simple straight lines and zigzags, sometimes without marking or with minimal marking. Use a quilter's ruler and marker to draw straight lines directly on the fabric as required. Lines can be quilted in embroidery stitches (see Quilter's Briefcase).

▶ Quilt wavy lines and simple motifs drawn freehand (see

Double Bottle Bag variation). Patterns can be improvized and drawn directly on to the fabric.

▶ Quilt patterns marked on the patchwork (see Victorian Circle Bag). These require marking by tracing the pattern from the illustration given and using dressmaker's carbon paper or Chaco chalk paper to transfer the design to the fabric. Alternatively, use the traditional English method and make a set of card or plastic templates to draw around.

▶ Making a Quilt Sandwich

After marking the quilt pattern you can prepare the quilt sandwich. Press the patchwork and backing fabric. Place the backing right side down on a flat surface and use masking tape to tape it down. Lay the wadding (batting) on top and smooth it out. Remember to match your wadding to the quilting technique you want to use – some wadding made for machine quilting is not suitable for hand quilting and vice versa (see wadding, page 92). Place the patchwork on top, making

sure there is wadding and backing behind all the patchwork. Tack (baste) the three layers together, working from the centre outwards in a radiating pattern. This method is suitable for the small pieces of quilting used in bags. Diagonal tacking anchors the layers together even more firmly and is easier to remove after machine quilting (see Stitch Library page 112). Alternatively, pin the layers together, but take care when machine sewing over pins. Once the quilt sandwich has been prepared, you are ready to quilt – machine quilting and hand quilting techniques are described below and on the following pages.

▶ Machine Quilting

Machine quilting (left in photo overleaf) gives a distinct line which can be used to emphasize the patchwork by quilting 'in the ditch' or along the patchwork seam line, on the other side of the seam from the patchwork seam allowance. Machine quilt in a graphic style with a darker thread or use invisible nylon thread if you don't want to see the stitches. If your machine has embroidery or interesting utility stitches, experiment with these for quilting.

I work with the machine feed dogs set 'up', use a slightly longer stitch length than average and quilt in continuous lines. Unlike quilting a large quilt, which should begin in the centre, starting and finishing at the edge of a small patchwork means there are fewer loose ends to finish off. Working this way and stitching slowly I did not need to use a walking foot to quilt. If the top fabric makes a little bump immediately in front of the presser foot, raise the foot and use the point of a pin to ease the fabric under. Make sure the needle is down in the fabric before raising the presser foot to turn corners. Follow gentle curves by raising the presser foot and turning the fabric slightly

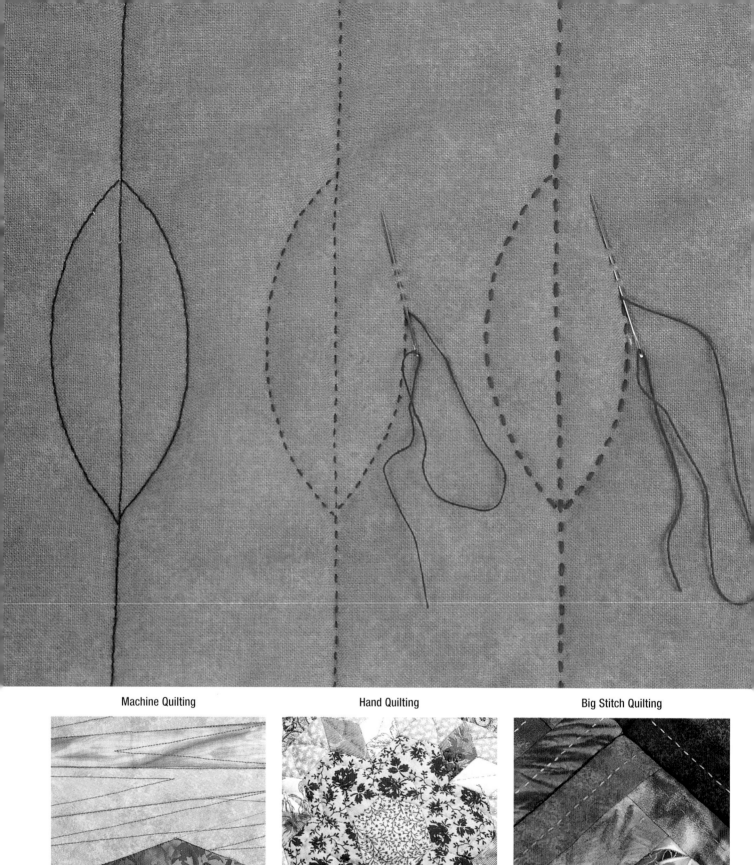

Machine Quilting

Hand Quilting

Big Stitch Quilting

after every couple of stitches. Freestyle machine quilting, worked with the machine feed dogs set 'down', requires practice to achieve good results – but if you enjoy quilting freestyle, use your own designs.

Some machines can stitch on the spot to finish off the thread ends or you could sew the last few stitches with a very short stitch length. In these bags, the back of the quilting is always hidden by the lining or bag construction, so loose ends can be pulled through to the back and knotted off.

▶ Hand Quilting

Hand quilting (centre in photo on left) gives a softer appearance than machine quilting. The aim is to have evenly spaced stitches rather than really tiny ones (see starting hand quilting, below). Traditional quilting in a frame helps to keep the layers taut and the quilting even. I didn't use a frame to quilt any of the bags as the patchwork pieces were small and were easier to work in the hand. If you want to use a frame, machine tack (baste) scrap pieces of fabric to each edge of the piece you want to quilt, so you have fabric to anchor the work in the frame. There are various kinds of smaller quilting frames and hoops available, some with clips to hold the work in place. Needles for hand quilting are called betweens and are smaller than sharps. If you work without a frame, you may find a small sharp easier to use but make sure your tension doesn't pucker up your quilting.

▶ Big Stitch Quilting

'Big stitch' is a variation on hand quilting, using thicker thread and larger stitches (right in photo on left). Use a crewel or embroidery needle suitable for the thread. Big stitch can enhance the colours in your patchwork and introduce multicoloured threads or metallics in an interesting way.

Starting hand quilting

Cut a thread about 18in long (shorter for embroidery threads and metallics) and tie a knot in one end, leaving a 'tail' about ½in long. Thread the needle. Insert the needle into the front of the work about ¾in along the line you are going to quilt and bring the needle up to start stitching. Gently pull the knot through the fabric and into the wadding (batting) and start stitching along the line. The 'tail' will be following the quilted line and be anchored by your first few stitches. Take small, neat stitches – loading three to four stitches on the needle keeps straight lines straight.

Finishing hand quilting

Make a knot about ¼in from the fabric surface. Take a backstitch, insert the needle along the line you have quilted and pull the knot into the wadding (batting). For extra secure finishing, tie two knots ¼in apart – these are very unlikely to work their way out of the quilting.

Neaten the edges of patchwork panels after quilting, before assembling your bag, by overlocking – check your machine for suitable stitches.

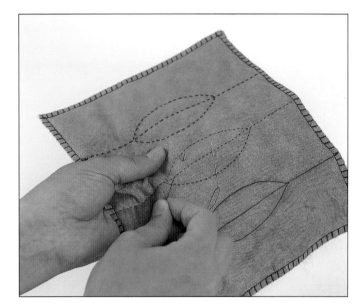

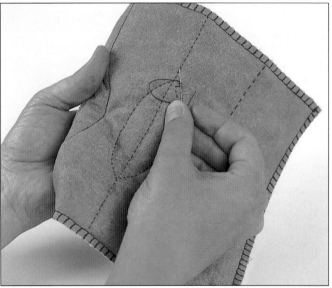

Matching quilting threads to needles
Match the type of quilting thread you want to use to your needle for best results.

Thread Type	Needle Type
Cotton hand quilting thread	Between or sharp
Embroidery threads (perlé, flower thread etc.)	Crewel or embroidery
Metallic embroidery threads	Crewel
Machine quilting	Medium universal
Jeans topstitch (machine)	Jeans
Rayon embroidery (machine)	Embroidery
Metallic embroidery (machine)	Metallic

Bag Making Techniques

Once your patchwork and quilting is complete you can assemble your bag. The project instructions give these details while this section describes the general bag making techniques required, including binding fabric edges, inserting zips, creating straps and making linings.

▶ *Making Bindings*

It is easy to make your own straight or bias bindings to co-ordinate with or match your bag. Use straight bindings (cut from the straight grain) where a firm straight edge is needed, such as the top of a pocket. Use bias binding where the edge has curves or curved corners. Double bindings are easiest to make and sew and are stronger in wear than single bindings. Take care not to stretch bias binding when easing around corners. Bias strips can also be used to make co-ordinated covered piping.

1 Cut 2in wide fabric strips to the length required. Straight grain strips will have a little stretch if cut across the fabric, from selvage to selvage. Cut bias strips at 45 degrees, using the 45-degree angle on your quilter's ruler. Larger bags will require joining pieces of binding. Both straight and bias bindings should be joined at a 45-degree angle. Cross the two strips and mark a stitching line, then machine sew. Trim off the excess fabric and press the seam open.

2 Fold the binding almost in half lengthways and press the fold in place. This way both raw edges of the binding are visible as it is pinned and sewn in place, so any puckers in the fabric underneath can be eased out. Clip off the 'dog ears'.

3 Pin the binding to the edge of the patchwork panel, raw edge to raw edge, as described in the individual bag project. Set the bias binding slightly back from the patchwork edge, so all the layers are visible and any puckers can be eased

out. Machine sew the binding in place, leaving about 4in of binding unsewn at the start and finish to make joining easier. Open out the folded binding and join the ends with a 45-degree angle, as in step 1. Refold the binding and finish sewing it to the panel.

4 Turn the binding to the back and stitch down using blind hemming stitch. Take care not to twist the binding.

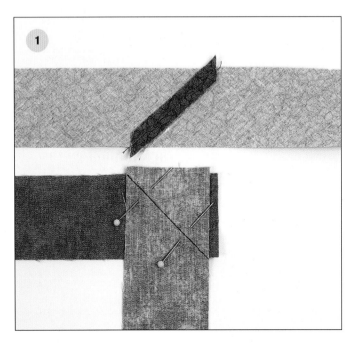

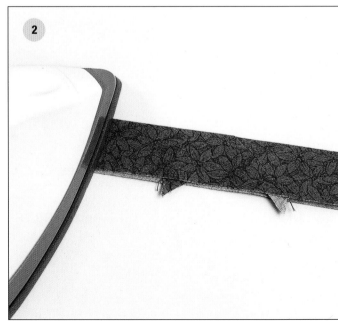

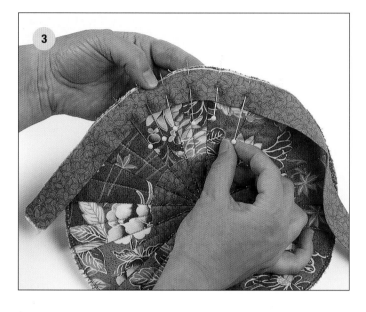

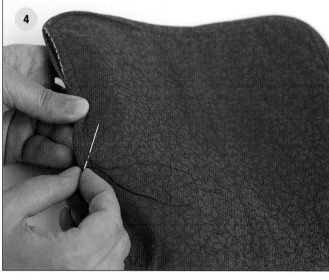

▶ *Inserting Zips*

About half the bags have zip fasteners, inserted by two basic methods. Either method can be used for bags where the zip is inserted into a gusset, such as the Small Workbag, Quilter's Briefcase or Zipover Rucksack. Use the invisible method, used in dressmaking, where the zip is sewn into the main part of the bag, as in the Rice Sack Bag. Tack (baste) zips in place with diagonal tacking as it is easier to remove after machine stitching. Bar tacks at either end of zips make it more secure (see Stitch Library page 112).

Allow ½in seam allowances for zips. Machine sew with a zipper foot to allow stitching close to the zip teeth. Take care not to sew over the teeth, which can break the needle. I sew with the zip open whenever possible. Stop sewing at the zip pull with the needle down in the fabric, draw the pull past the part being sewn and continue stitching. Zips can also be sewn by hand.

Inserting a visible zip

1 Fold under the first piece of fabric ½in and pin to the zip. The folded edge should be close to the teeth but allow the zip to be unfastened. Machine sew down the edge about ⅛in

from the fold. Sew the second piece of fabric to the zip the same way.

2 Cut fabric to equal the total width of the zip gusset. Machine sew to the end of the zip gusset.

3 Cut fabric for the other end of the zip gusset and machine sew. Press end pieces outwards. Trim gusset to required length.

Calculating fabric sizes for zip gussets

If you want to adapt a bag you may need to change the size of the zip gusset using the information here (see also adapting bags page 111).

▶ **For a bag with a visible zip gusset:**

Long pieces (cut 2):
To calculate the length of the fabric: add ½in to the length of the zip.
To calculate the width of the fabric: subtract the width of the zip teeth (approximately ¼in) from the width of gusset, divide by 2 and add ¾in (¼in normal seam allowance and ½in for zip edge).

End pieces (cut 2):
To calculate the length of the fabric: subtract the length of the zip gusset after step 1 from the desired finished length, divide the result by 2 and add ¾in.
To calculate the width of the fabric: measure the width of the zip gusset after step 1.

▶ **For a bag with an unlined visible zip gusset:**

Long pieces (cut 2):
To calculate the length of the fabric: (to be folded in half lengthways at start of step 1) add ¼in to the length of the zip tape.
To calculate the width of the fabric: subtract the width of the zip teeth (approximately ¼in) from the width of the gusset and add ½in.

End pieces (cut 2):
As for visible zip gusset, or cut four and sew a piece to each side of the zip gusset in steps 2 and 3 to conceal all raw edges when finished.

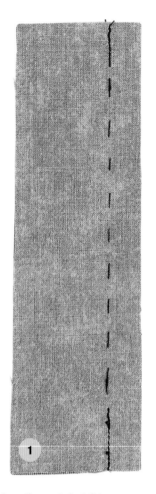

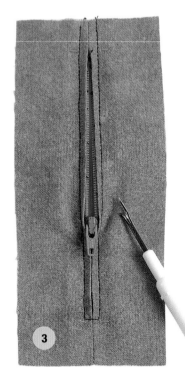

Inserting a zip invisibly

1 With a ½in seam allowance, machine (or hand) sew both ends of the zip gusset, starting and finishing with backstitches. Tack (baste) the remaining opening closed.

2 Press seam open. Diagonally tack zip in place from the back.

3 Machine (or hand) sew the zip from the right side of work, removing tacking (basting) and opening the zip as required. Check that the zip opens and remove tacking holding the zip in place. The ends of the zip opening can be reinforced with a bar tack.

a

b

c

▶ Making Straps

The most basic strap is a single piece of strong webbing. Three other strap methods use fabric to match the bag. Remember that fabric tends to stretch across the grain, from selvage to selvage, so always cut the strap parallel to the selvage.

Tube strap (a)

Cut a strip of fabric to the desired length (finished length + ½in) and width (double the finished width + ½in). Fold the fabric wrong sides together and machine sew along one side. Turn the strap right side out and press with the seam to one side. Narrow straps in thick fabric or with wadding (batting) are more difficult to turn right side out.

Padded strap (b)

Cut fabric as if making a tube strap and cut a strip of wadding (batting) the same size as the finished length and width.

Tack (baste) the wadding to the fabric, ¼in from the long edge, fold the fabric over and machine sew in place. Remove the tacking.

Folded strap (c)

This method can be used for webbing that would be too thin to use on its own. Cut a strip of fabric to the

desired length (finished length + ½in) and double the finished width, which must be the same as or wider than the webbing. Cut a piece of webbing the same length as the fabric. Fold the fabric edges towards the centre and press in place. Machine sew the webbing along the length of the strap.

Attaching straps and D-rings (d)

Straps can be sewn directly to a bag (see Rice Sack Bag) or attached with D-rings (see Victorian Circle Bag). Attach the strap securely by machine sewing a figure of eight. To sew the strap directly to a bag, fold under the ends of the strap and stitch. The fold may be omitted and the strap ends covered with a piece of appliqué (see Batik Satchel). The bag can also be reinforced at this point with a piece of strong calico on the inside. Use the same figure of eight stitching to attach straps to D-rings and clips. Thread the strap through the D-ring or the bar on the clip, fold the raw edge under and machine sew.

▶ Making Linings

All the bags, with the exception of the reversible Inside Outside bag, have linings. The basic linings, without pockets, are cut to the same sizes as the outer bag panels. The easiest way to cut the linings accurately is to use the outer panels as cutting patterns, before the bag is assembled. Very thin lining fabrics, such as waterproof nylon, may be semi-transparent and will need an interlining sewn to the back. Slipstitching the lining to the bag along the seam lines, working from

inside the bag, helps to keep the lining in place at the top of the Zipover Rucksack and the Small Workbag. Topstitching around the edge of bags like the Tough Tote keeps the join between bag and lining crisply folded.

▶ Adding Extra Pockets

Many of the bags have pockets and the various types used are described in the projects but if you wish to add extra pockets or customize your bag interior or further adapt the designs, the following advice should help.

To add an extra pocket, first make a sketch of the lining, note the dimensions and mark where you would like to add the pocket.

For a pocket the same width as

your lining, follow the assembly directions for the Quilter's Briefcase lining, page 47. Cut the pocket as wide as the lining and any length you wish, shorter than the side of the bag.

For a self-lined patch pocket, decide the size of the pocket and cut out an extra piece of lining twice that size. Fold it in half, right sides together and sew around the edge leaving a 2in gap. Bag out, slipstitch the gap closed and machine sew the patch pocket to the lining, reinforcing the lining behind the pocket stitching with a piece of calico slightly larger than the pocket.

To insert zip pockets in the lining, follow the directions for the Quilter's Travel Bag on page 28. Remember that the pocket fabric will be the same width as the lining.

If you want a lot of pockets or loops, like the inside of the Small Workbag (shown below), split the lining up into different elements. Divide your lining plan into rectangles and squares, rather like making an asymmetric patchwork block and think of each element like a piece for patchwork. Add the pockets and loops to each piece and assemble the lining like a patchwork, catching the ends of the loops and edges of the pockets into the lining seams. You can add pockets for mobile phones, diaries and other small items this way or add a loop for your key ring.

Adapting Bags

If you want a design challenge, any of the bags in this book can be a starting point for a unique creation!

▶ At the simplest level, alter the fabrics and patchwork elements (see Block Library for ideas).

▶ Change straps and fastenings.

▶ Add or remove pockets.

▶ Change the bag size. Decide how large you would like it to be, remembering to think three-dimensionally. Making a sketch and drawing a plan on squared paper helps. If a bag is to accommodate a particular cutting board or sketchbook, check the size. The fabric requirements in the bag instructions are given without seam allowances to make resizing easier, so remember to add seam allowances when you cut out the pieces. Mark the position and size of patchwork panels on your plan and list the dimensions of all the pieces – this will be your cutting list. You will also need to change the length of zips and straps. Several bags have curved corners sewn to a gusset, so check the circumference of the curve and allow for this when calculating the length of the gusset panels. The original bag assembly instructions may need to be amended with extra steps, if you wish add a pocket for example.

Stitch Library

Various hand stitches were used in the construction of the bags including backstitch, bar tacking, diagonal tacking, hemming stitch, running stitch and whipstitch. Decorative embroidery stitches were used for embellishment on some of the bags. I used machine embroidery but you may prefer to embroider by hand and so diagrams for blanket stitch, chain stitch, feather stitch, herringbone stitch and stem stitch are included here. The stitches are presented in alphabetical order, with letter sequences showing their formation where appropriate.

Backstitch

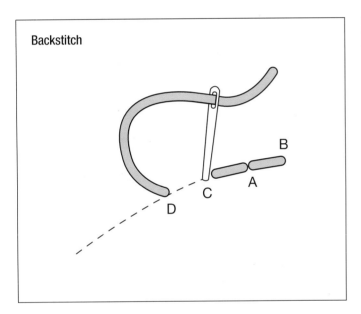

Bar tacking

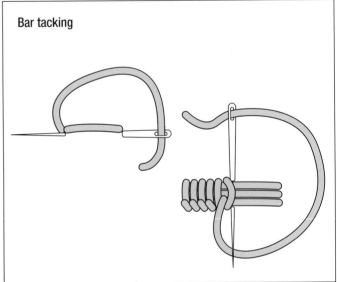

Blanket stitch

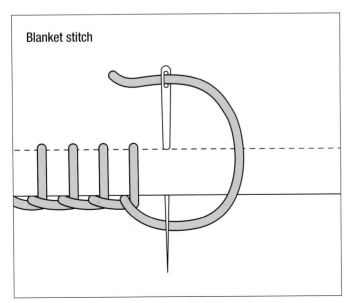

Chain stitch

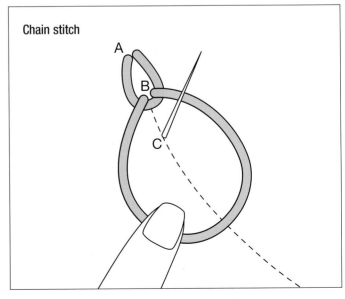

Diagonal tacking

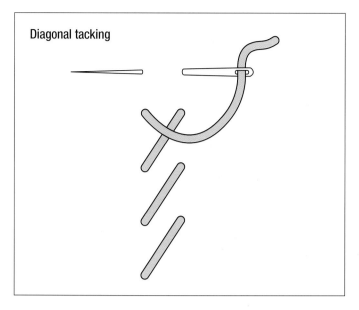

Feather stitch

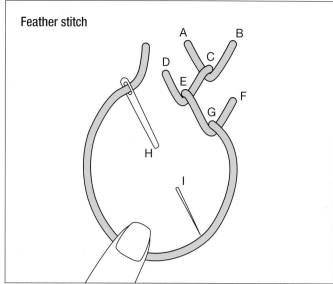

Hemming stitch

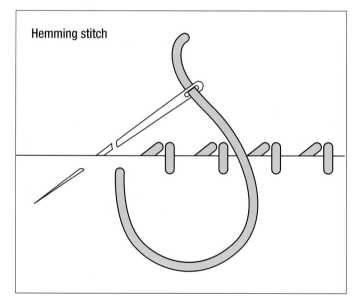

Herringbone stitch

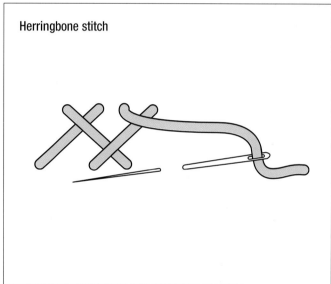

Stem stitch

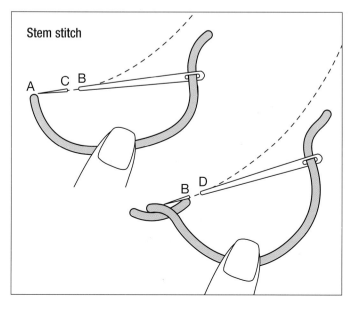

Whipstitch

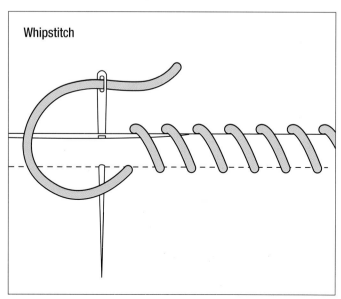

Fabric Themes

Small projects are a great opportunity to play around with fabric colours and themes, without the commitment of a large quilt. You can use up fabrics from your scrap bag or experiment with new fabrics and novelty prints. As the bags in this book show, you can complement your patchwork with fabrics like denim, needlecord or lightweight furnishings where piecing is not required. Try using buttons and other notions to enhance your theme. Embroidery and big stitch quilting can further embellish your bags. I used ten themes, echoing a wide range of styles and colourways.

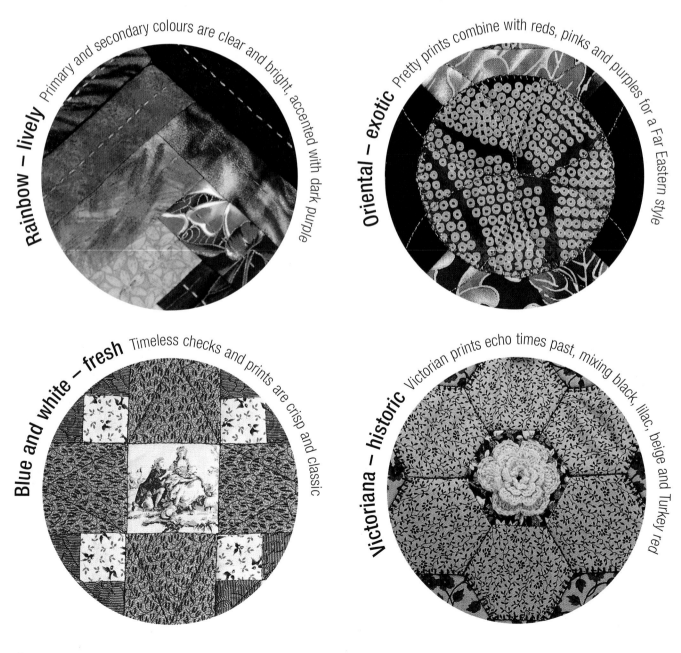

Rainbow – lively Primary and secondary colours are clear and bright, accented with dark purple

Oriental – exotic Pretty prints combine with reds, pinks and purples for a Far Eastern style

Blue and white – fresh Timeless checks and prints are crisp and classic

Victoriana – historic Victorian prints echo times past, mixing black, lilac, beige and Turkey red

Landscape – natural Countryside colours, leaf and landscape prints, reflect the great outdoors

Country – homely Visit the farm with essential denim and checks, plus novelty chicken prints

Winter festivals – cosy Celebration red, burgundy, green and gold prints hint of snow, stars and frost

Africa – vibrant Large batik prints, ikat weaves and earthy shades evoke the continent's rich colours

1930s – nostalgic Nursery prints, Art Deco colours and 'feed sack' florals mix for a retro look

Romance – delicate Silks, gold prints and mother-of-pearl buttons evoke old-fashioned valentines

Block Library

This library features some of my favourite blocks, and along with those used in the bags, should give you plenty of design options. They can be made with combinations of various patchwork techniques described in the previous pages. There are exploded diagrams of some blocks to help you plan the number of pieces and various units required to make them. All are suitable for machine piecing. The blocks are grouped into three sizes – 4in, 6in and 8in – the sizes used in the bags. They are also grouped into four-patch and nine-patch designs.

Four Inch Blocks

Four-patch blocks are easiest to use where the finished block size can be divided by two and are shown here as 4in blocks. Nine-patch blocks are suited to finished sizes divisible by three and are shown as 6in blocks. Rail Fence is not really a nine-patch but works better in the same sizes. The 8in blocks would also work as 4in blocks, but would have small pieces such as ½in strips. It's possible to use blocks in other sizes that don't divide so easily but you will have pieces sized in fractions of an inch. The blocks here have been reduced to fit, so you will need to scale them up to the right size.

Combinations of colour and pattern are infinite and quilters have an enormous variety to choose from. Consider the effects of colour and pattern when you select your patchwork fabrics. Stripes can make an interesting design feature and large prints look very different when cut up (see Rice Sack Bag variation). Strong tonal contrasts and the use of opposite colours, such as blue and orange, make bold patchwork patterns, while small prints and low contrast can soften the pieced effect.

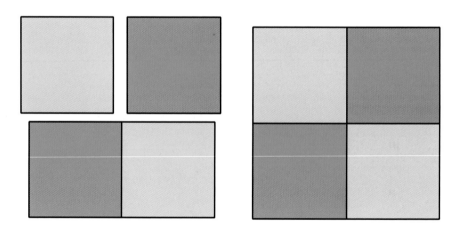

Basic four-patch block

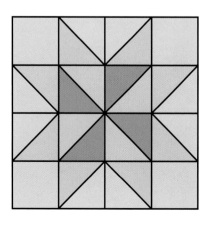

Pieced Star

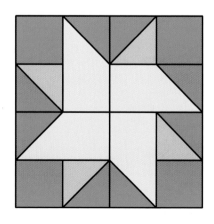

Pale Star

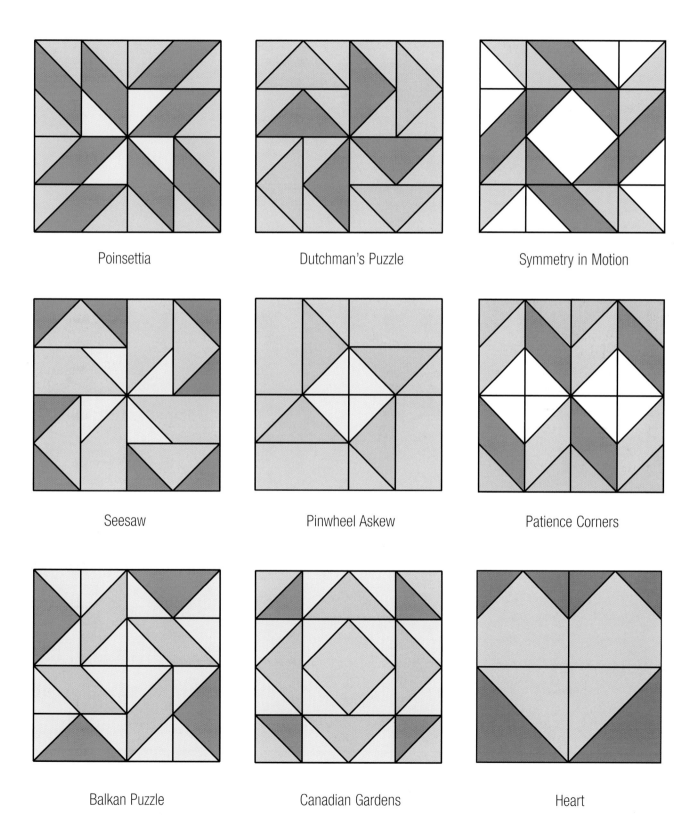

Poinsettia

Dutchman's Puzzle

Symmetry in Motion

Seesaw

Pinwheel Askew

Patience Corners

Balkan Puzzle

Canadian Gardens

Heart

Six Inch Blocks

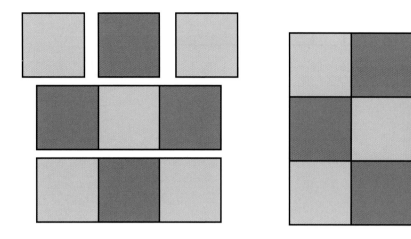

Basic nine-patch block

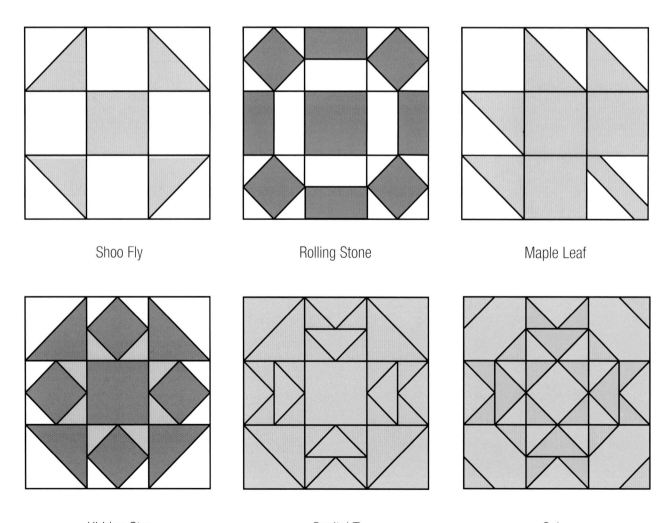

Shoo Fly

Rolling Stone

Maple Leaf

Hidden Star

Capital T

Salem

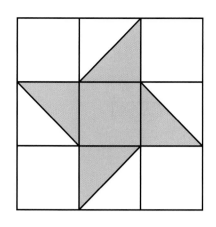

Friendship Star

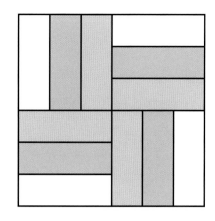

Rail Fence

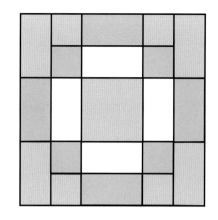

Antique Tile

Eight Inch Blocks

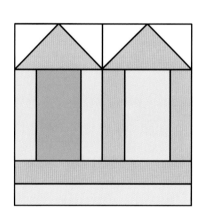

Beach Huts

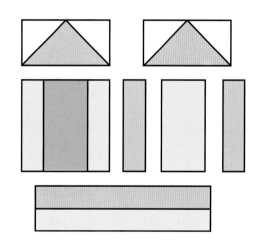

Beach Huts construction

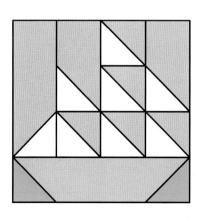

Sailing Ship

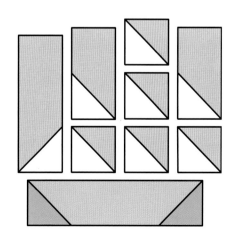

Sailing Ship construction

Suppliers

UK Suppliers

* Mail order and quilt shows only

The African Fabric Shop *

19 Hebble Mount
Meltham
Holmfirth
West Yorkshire HD9 4HG
tel: 01484 850188
email: maggie.relph@virgin.net
*Fabrics including wax prints, Gambian batiks
and 'Three Cats' prints from South Africa*

The Button Lady *

16 Hollyfield Road South
Sutton Coldfield
West Midlands B76 1NX
tel: 0121 329 3234
*Buttons and clasps in all styles and materials;
charms, beads and sequins; soft leather pieces*

The Cotton Patch

1285 Stratford Road
Hall Green
Birmingham B28 9AJ
tel: 0121 702 2840
email: mailorder@cottonpatch.net
*Wide range of fabrics, wadding (batting),
notions and equipment*

Creative Grids

71 Westfield Road
Leicester
Leicestershire LE3 6HU
tel: 0116 285 7151
email: creativegrids@btinternet.com
*Quilt rulers and mats, also wadding (batting)
and general equipment*

Euro Japan Links Limited *

32 Nant Road
Childs Hill
London NW1 2AT
tel: 020 8201 9324
email: eurojpn@aol.com
*Traditional and modern Japanese fabrics
(including thicker cottons), sashiko threads
and other materials*

US Suppliers

The City Quilter

157 West 24th Street
New York, NY 1011
tel: 212-807-0390
*Wide range of fabrics, wadding (batting),
notions and equipment
(shop and mail order)*

Connecting Threads

13118 NE 4th Street
Vancouver
tel: 1-800 574 6454
email: customerservice@connectingthreads.com
website: www.connectingthreads.com
For general needlework and quilting supplies

Joann Stores, Inc

5555 Darrow Road
Hudson, Ohio
tel: 1-888 739 4120
email: guestservice@jo-annstores.com
website: www.joann.com
*For general needlework and quilting supplies (mail
order and shops across the US)*

Keepsake Quilting

Route 25B
Center Harbor, NH
tel: 1-800 865 9458
email: customerservice@keepsakequilting.com
website: www.keepsakequilting.com
For general needlework and quilting supplies

Acknowledgments

I would like to thank everyone who contributed to the creation of *21 Terrific Patchwork Bags*. Special thanks to my commissioning editor Cheryl Brown, my art editor Alison Myer, desk editor Sandra Pruski, project editor Lin Clements, all the team at David and Charles and photographer Lucy Mason for helping to turn my idea for the book into reality – you have all been great to work with and incredibly patient!

I am grateful to Val Shields for assistance with bag assembly for the step-by-step photo shoots and Susan Hill for her meticulous English paper pieced samples. A very, very big 'thank you' goes to Howard Bogod at Bernina UK for the wonderful Virtuosa 153 Quilter's Edition sewing machine, which has made sewing the bags a great pleasure – it has stitched beautifully on all kinds of fabrics. Many thanks to Susan Pitt at Concord Makower fabrics for gorgeous prints (including the chickens!). Many thanks also to the Cotton Patch and Euro Japan Links who supplied the 1930s reproduction cottons and Japanese print fabrics respectively – two of my favourite fabric themes.

Finally, thank you to my family and all my friends in patchwork and quilting for your support and encouragement. I hope you enjoy this book.

Index

Page numbers in *italic* type refer to illustrations.

A
Antique Tile *119*
appliqué 17, 33, 35, 102, *102*
  circles 72–3, *72–3*
  fusible web 23, *23*, 102
  hand 102, *102*
  landscape scenes 43
  needleturn 102, *102*
Art Deco 61

B
backing fabrics 91, 103
backstitch *112*
Balkan Puzzle 117
bar tack 67, *112*
Batik Satchel **76–81**, 98
batting *see* wadding
beach bags 91
Beach Hut 36–41, *119*
beads 94, 102
bias binding 47, 60, 106, *106*
big stitch quilting 23, *23*, 55, *55*, 78, *78*, 104, 105, *105*
bindings 106, *106*
blanket stitch *112*
blended wadding 92
blocks 95, *116–19*
braid 102
briefcase 42–9
broderie anglaise 16
button loops 7
buttons 92, 94, 102

C
Canadian Gardens 12–17, 14, *117*
Capital T *118*
carbon paper 103
Chaco chalk paper 103
chain piecing 97
chain stitch *112*
chainette loops 75, *75*
charm patchwork 74
Churn Dash 63, 64, *64*, 98
colourwash effect 79
cords 7, 93–4
cotton à broder 92
cotton fabrics 91
cotton wadding 92
cutting mat 88, 96, *96*

D
D-rings and clips 94, 110, *110*
Delectable Mountains 51, 52–3, *52–3*
diagonal tacking *113*
diamonds 32–3, 102, *102*
Double Bottle Bag *18–23*
drawstring bag 70–5
Dutchman's Puzzle *117*

E
Eight Point Star 25, *26*, 55, *55*, 99
embroidery 102
embroidery stitch quilting 103
embroidery threads 92, 105
English paper piecing 17, 30–5, *101–2*, 101–2, 103
Envelope Bag **6–11**, 99
equipment 88–90

F
fabric themes *114–15*
fabrics 91
  cutting 96, *96*
  preparation 96
Fair and Square 12–17, *14*
Fan Purse **56–61**, 99, 100–1
fasteners 92–3
fat eighth 91
fat quarter 91
feather stitch *113*
Flying Geese 14, 25, *27*, 98–9
folded strap 109–10, *109*
foundation piecing 34, 43–5, *44–5*, 56–7, *57*, 82–5, *84–5*, 99–101, *100–1*
four-patch blocks 116, *116–17*
frame, quilting 105
freestyle machine quilting 105
Friendship Star *119*
furoshiki 19
fusible web 102

G
grain, fabric 11
Grandmother's Flower Garden 101

H
hand quilting *104*, 105
Heart *117*
hemming stitch *113*
hexagons 17, 30–5, 101, *101*, *102*
Hidden Star *118*
hoop, quilting 105

I
in the ditch quilting 103
Inside Outside Bag **70–5**
invisible thread 92, 103

J
jeans thread 92, 105

L
landscape scenes 42–9, 82–6
large-print patterns 79, 116
leather 81
linings 91, 110–11
Log Cabin 6–11, *8–9*, 100, *100*
  foundation piecing 60, *60*, 83
Long Workbag **36–41**
loop-and-ball fasteners 92

M
machine piecing 97, *97*
machine quilting 12–17, 18–23, 56–9, 72, 92, 103, *104*, 105
make-up bag 61
Maple Leaf *118*
markers 90, 103
materials 91–4
metallic thread 19, 56, 70, 72, 92, 105

N
needles 90
nine-patch blocks 116, *118–19*
nylon thread 92, 103

P
Pale Star *116*
parachute clips 93
Patience Corners *117*
pens, fabric 23
Pieced Star *116*
pins, quilting 90
Pinwheel *77–9*, *78–9*, 98
Pinwheel Askew *117*
piping 13, 16–17, *16*, 94
pockets 110–11
  taping 47
  zip 110
Poinsettia *117*
polyester wadding 92
popper fasteners 94
presser feet 90, *90*
pressing patchwork 97, *97*
print pattern, quilting following 103

Q
quick unpick 90
quilt sandwich 103
Quilter's Briefcase **42–9**
Quilter's Travel Bag **24–9**, 98, 99
quilting pattern, marking 103
quilting techniques 103–5

R
Rail Fence 116, *119*
Rainbow Bag **11**
rayon thread 92, 105
Rice Sack Bag **62–7**, 99
Rolling Stone *118*
rotary cutter 88, 96, *96*
rucksack 82–7
ruler, quilter's 88, 90, 96, *96*
running stitch *113*

S
safety 96
Sailing Ship 36–41, *119*
Salem *118*
sashiko 77, 92
satchel 76–81
scissors 90

seam allowance 95
  thick fabrics 79
seam ripper 90
Seesaw *117*
Seminole patchwork 97–8, *98*
sequins 94
sewing machine 90
shaded thread 23, *23*, 55, *55*, 105
Shoo Fly *118*
silk fabrics 9, 91
Small Workbag **50–5**
Snowball 99
stem stitch *113*
stitch and flip strip 99, 100
stitch library *112–13*
straps
  attachment 110
  folded 109–10, *109*
  padded 109, *109*
  tube 109, *109*
  webbing 12–17, 29, 93
stripes 116
Symmetry in Motion *117*
synthetic fabrics 91

T
techniques 95–111
templates, ready-made 90
text messages 23
thick fabrics 79
threads 91–2
Thrifty 63, 64, *64*
toggles 92
toile de Jouy 13, 15
tonal contrast 116
tote bag **12–17**
Tough Tote 12–17
travel bag 24–9
triangle squares 70–5, *72*, 98, *98*, 99
triangles 11
tube strap 109, *109*
Tumbling Blocks 102

V
Victorian Circle Bag **30–5**, 101
Victorian Print Tote **17**

W
wadding 92, 103
waterproof linings 61, 91
webbing straps and handles 12–17, 29, 93
whipstitch *113*
wool wadding 92

Z
Zipover Rucksack **82–7**
zips 92–3
  inserting 107–8, *107–8*
  pulls 54